VERSES AND MEDITATION

VERSES AND MEDITATIONS

RUDOLF STEINER

*With an Introduction and Notes
by George Adams*

RUDOLF STEINER PRESS

Translation revised by D.S. Osmond and C. Davy

Rudolf Steiner Press
Hillside House, The Square
Forest Row, RH18 5ES

www.rudolfsteinerpress.com

Published by Rudolf Steiner Press 2004

First published in English in 1961

The original German verses are drawn from the *Rudolf Steiner Gesamtausgabe* (or Collected Works) published by Rudolf Steiner Verlag, Dornach. These authorized translations are published by permission of the Rudolf Steiner Nachlassverwaltung, Dornach

Translation © Rudolf Steiner Press 1961

A catalogue record for this book is available from the British Library

ISBN 1 85584 197 5

Cover by Andrew Morgan Design
Printed and bound in Great Britain by Cromwell Press Limited, Trowbridge, Wilts.

CONTENTS

INTRODUCTION

Many people in our time are looking for a more conscious spiritual pathway—a method of mental and spiritual training which is to open the human mind and soul to the Divine creative Spirit that underlies the Universe in which we live, while at the same time rendering us by self-mastery, by the control of thought and the refinement of our life of feeling, more efficient in our daily tasks, more truly sensitive and helpful in our relations with our fellow-men.

It is well known that in the Orient methods and schools of spiritual training have existed since time immemorial; they are part of the very fabric of Eastern civilizations. Western people, looking for spiritual guidance in this sense, have therefore often naturally turned to Eastern sources. That this is happening to-day is also characteristic of the tendency of our time towards a greater universality—breaking down barriers between races, continents and cultural traditions, shewing more readiness to learn from one another, overcoming religious bigotry and national self-sufficiency. The tendency is welcome. Yet the traditional Eastern methods, directly transplanted, are not well adapted—either to the outward forms of Western life or to the mind and character of Western man. Moreover, in the West as in the East, though less in evidence, there exists a deeper spiritual stream, a mystical tradition.

7

In the lives of outstanding individuals—founders, for example, of religious and philosophic movements—in the great religious orders and in spiritual fraternities less widely known, the "Path of Knowledge" and the meditative life have been pursued.

It is as a spiritual being that man creates civilization of whatsoever kind. No civilization can exist unless founded on the aspiration towards, and on the wisdom that flows out of, the spiritual world. External and materialistic as it may seem to be, this applies also to the scientific civilization of modern Europe and America. The beginnings of Science were part of a deep and many-sided spiritual movement at the time of the Renaissance. The early scientists—those for example who, in London in the 17th century, used to meet at "Gresham College" (forming the nucleus of what was then to become the Royal Society)—thought of themselves as "experimental philosophers". Among them were men for whom the new method of putting questions to Nature was part of a far wider spiritual quest.

The Science that was then begun has by the 20th century led to a situation in which modern man has need of greater spiritual forces. Having penetrated deeply into Nature, unlocking many of her secrets on the material and sub-material plane, he needs to restore the balance—to take a comparable forward step in his inner life, and to gain access to those hidden aspects of Nature which require more than intellectual faculties for their discernment. This indeed grows more urgently necessary with every technical advance and with every passing year. A wider spiritual range, a deeper poise of the inner life, are needed now than when our outer forms of production—even a hundred years ago, long after the machine age had begun—were at a vastly more primitive level than they are to-day.

Rudolf Steiner was the teacher of a method of self-education and spiritual awakening in keeping with and, in many ways, a direct outcome of the scientific age— in continuity with the ideals out of which it began its growth four or five hundred years ago. It is a method applicable by men and women fully engaged in all the tasks and avocations of our time. It does not call for any kind of withdrawal from practical life in the modern world; rather the contrary, it helps one enter into it more wholeheartedly, more fully. It contains elements in common with Eastern traditions, but they are trans-muted—re-born in a Western setting and in accordance with Western needs. At the same time it is deeply imbued with the esoteric substance of Christianity— Christianity not in any denominational sense but as a living experience in the midst of present-day realities.

The very titles of Rudolf Steiner's fundamental works bear witness to what has here been said. For example: *Mysticism at the Dawn of Modern Time and its relation to the Scientific Outlook, Christianity as Mystical Fact and the Mysteries of Antiquity*, lectures on the Gospel of

St. John and on the three Synoptic Gospels, *Theosophy: an Introduction to the Supersensible Knowledge of the World and the Destination of Man, An Outline of Occult Science, Knowledge of the Higher Worlds and its Attainment.* It is in this latter work above all that he describes the kind of spiritual discipline which a modern man may undertake, leading to the purification and enhancement of his faculties and calling forth the deeper powers of cognition by which he will gain direct insight into the hidden spiritual background of all life.

The opening passages of the book reveal the character and tendency of the path here recommended. It is "the path of veneration, of devotion for truth and knowledge". The student—or, to use more old-fashioned words, the aspirant, the disciple—needs to develop reverence towards the manifestations of the world in which he finds himself. He is not to suppress his critical faculties, still less his independent judgment, but he must be aware that it is reverence and devotion which will open the eyes of the soul. What you do not revere, what you cannot love and thankfully receive, will not reveal itself to you. The method then set forth contains the following components. It includes at an early stage the thoughtful contemplation of Nature—of the rocks and crystals in the mineral kingdom; the growing and decaying plant, the seed and the future plant that will arise therefrom; the animals with their inner life of craving, suffering and enjoyment; the sounds emitted

10

by animate creatures, such as the cry of the warm-blooded animal, and also inanimate sounds such as the ringing of a bell or the booming of the waves on the shore. The word "contemplation" is here used to cover both the thoughtful observation of the thing as it confronts one, and the reflection on what has once been seen or heard, evoked in memory and imagination while the exercise is being done. Sometimes it is the one, sometimes the other. A number of exercises of this kind are carefully described, each in its proper context, and it is characteristic that they occur above all in the opening chapters of the book. It is as though the writer were holding out his hand to the natural and healthy interests of modern man—his interest in the Earth-planet and in the land in which he lives, his love of animals both wild and domesticated, his enjoyment of the trees and flowers, the tilling of his garden. On one occasion, it is said, when a group of young men and women came to Dr. Steiner for conversation and advice (it was the time of the *Wandervogel* movement in Germany with its romantic idealization of Nature), he said to them among other things: "The way to get really near to Nature is given in the book *Knowledge of the Higher Worlds and its Attainment.*"

Another essential feature is the taking in hand of one's own daily life, in the development of ethical qualities such as patience, tolerance, thankfulness, positiveness towards others, the "listening" attitude, the overcoming of hidden prejudices, the readiness to learn afresh at every moment. In this respect Rudolf Steiner does not give "counsels of perfection", but he points out that life is constantly giving us opportunities to develop these qualities and that we can set about it in a quite practical way, sometimes deliberately devoting attention to one thing at a time. He does not so much exhort, but quietly describes the several effects of these qualities in the development of the soul's organs of cognition; the hindering effect of their opposite. Above all, he is insistent that other exercises on the path to higher knowledge may produce harmful results if this aspect is neglected. He gives it as the golden rule: "For every one step that you take in the pursuit of Higher Knowledge, take three in the development of your character towards the Good." For example, the thoughtful contemplation of Nature might well be held to include human nature, and so in a sense it does, but here we ourselves are involved in quite another way. We have to perceive, with growing clarity of discernment, the manifestations of mind and soul in our fellow-men, but we can only do so truly and without offence inasmuch as we ourselves are growing in self-knowledge, and above all, inasmuch as we revere and respect the sacredness of individuality in every man.

A further feature of the spiritual path, closely related to the last, is the practice of looking back reflectively on the course of our own life. We should do this at longer intervals, surveying a whole period of our life, passing in review our aims, our failures and achievements, pondering on our resolves for the future. But we are also recommended to do it in a certain way from day to day. In his advice to individuals, Dr. Steiner generally recommended that in the evening, before going to sleep, one should spend five or ten minutes looking back on the events of the day with the calm eye of detachment. The exercise has many aspects. If rightly done it is bound to include thankfulness for the experiences and encounters which the day has brought. In this respect it has something in common with the evening prayer of a truly religious man. One is to do it thoughtfully, realizing one's mistakes and yet without giving way to remorse. Rather should one try to see oneself just in the same way as one sees the other participants in the events and scenes on which one is looking back. We thus acquire the habit of looking at ourselves with detachment, as from outside, "seeing ourselves as others see us". Objectivity towards our own failings as towards those of others, trust above all in the clarifying and ultimately strengthening effect of pure and quiet thought, was what Dr. Steiner inculcated. Though not in *Knowledge of the Higher Worlds*, in later writings and lectures and in his advice to individuals he recommended that in this exercise we begin with the evening and go back gradually to the morning. Definite reasons are given for thus "reversing" the flow of time.

A further component, related to this last and yet vividly distinguished from it, is the one with which the present volume is concerned, namely *Meditation* in the stricter sense. For even if, in the preceding exercise, we look upon our life with detachment and from a higher vantage-point, it is still the circumstances of our own particular life with which we are occupied. The human soul on its spiritual pathway has need of more than this. We need to enter into things of universal significance, things that belong to our ultimate origin and goal. These are the truths that concern us purely and simply as human beings, born of the eternal Spirit that under-lies all things that are. They would concern us equally whatever time and clime we belonged to; they relate us therefore to all Mankind, past and present and in the future.

Therefore the path of knowledge and of self-develop-ment also includes the regular practice of Meditation proper. In the sacred literature of all ages, says Rudolf Steiner, and in the gnostic, mystical and spiritual-scientific literature of our own time, the aspirant will find suitable contents for meditation, both in the form of words and in the imaginative or symbolic pictures that are given. Evening by evening, before or after the exercise of looking back on the day, five or ten minutes should be devoted to meditation on a chosen verse—or "mantram", to call it by the Eastern term frequently used by Dr. Steiner in this connection. And in the mornings too, as soon as practicable upon awakening or after getting up, a like period of time should be devoted to a suitably chosen meditation.

In this connection—and of course also in the looking back with detachment on the events of the day—very much depends on the effort of will that is put into it. Almost everyone (at least in the Western world) who has ever tried to meditate, will have discovered that the very resolve to do this—to enter, as the saying goes, "into the silence"—tends to bring stray thoughts crowding into the mind. It requires effort of will to put the stray thoughts aside—to give one's mind quietly and concentratedly to the chosen subject. It is this "bringing of will into one's thinking" which in the long run leads to the vitalizing of one's thoughts, till they no longer bear the "pale cast" they do in ordinary life, but are awakened into living and imaginative perception.

What is needed above all is unending patience and perseverance—the kind of perseverance which, having once recognized that the thing is good, will not be discouraged by repeated failures. The good will of the meditator—his faithfulness to himself, and therewith to the spiritual world, in holding to his resolve—comes to expression not only in the effort he puts into it every time he enters into meditation, but in the perseverance through the days and years, undaunted by many seeming failures. The failure in any case is generally not as great as it seems to oneself. The real progress one is making is delicate and subtle and often finds expression in quite other ways before one is aware of it directly. But without faithful perseverance nothing can be achieved.

For this reason, too, it is recommended that one goes on for a long time—for weeks or months or even years— from day to day with a once chosen morning and evening meditation (these will generally be distinct, though related); it is less good to be constantly changing. It is the beginner, rather than the one more advanced along the meditative path, who imagines that he needs frequent change.

In choosing a subject for regular meditation the great majority will feel the need of some help and guidance, and in this connection first and foremost the present volume is being published. For it contains, among other things, meditative verses given from time to time by Rudolf Steiner, either to individuals from whom these treasures have been bequeathed—most of them have long since passed away—or to one or other circle of his pupils. The book includes a wide selection to meet a diversity of individual needs. Once again, for those who are practising meditation the importance is emphasized of making a definite choice and abiding by it.

Before we go on to describe what the book contains, we should however mention one further aspect—also a very essential component—of the spiritual path as taught by Rudolf Steiner. It is the *study* of Spiritual Science, contained as this now is in a great variety of books—those above all by this great teacher himself. Needless to say, "study" will also take the form of joining in study-circles with others, hearing lectures and so on, but one's own quiet reading is not unimportant.

Spiritual Science, Gnosis, Theosophia, Anthroposophia—whatever name we may call it by—is the imparting of those great truths concerning the Divine origin of all things, the spiritual structure of the Universe in which we live, the evolution and future destiny above all of Man himself, which are perceived and experienced when the higher faculties of the soul have been developed. The seed of these faculties is there in all human souls. But there have lived, in every age, individuals in whom these faculties were already developed in a far higher degree than in the rest of mankind. Among these have been the founders of the great religions; the informers and instructors of the great impulses of civilization, such as the almost legendary figures of Zarathustra, Hermes and Orpheus in olden time; the authors or inspirers of the sacred writings of mankind. Among them, too, have been the Masters and Initiates, whose true character and presence among the masses of mankind are often veiled from outer sight, also the great Mystics and spiritual Philosophers, and such as are called Saints by the Western, Elders or Startzy by the Eastern Church,

Mahatmas in the oriental tradition. In many languages, in forms of expression pictorial or half-symbolical, in ritual and sacred drama, the great truths of the Spiritual World have been and are still being bequeathed to mankind, according to the needs of different epochs and populations. What we are calling "Spiritual Science" is at least one of the forms in which the spiritual truths are seeking to find expression in the language of our own time and in the mental climate of Western culture.

Now it might easily be thought: If the faculty to perceive these things is latent in us and we are rightly encouraged to develop it, let us by all means do so, and await what we shall see when our own powers of spiritual perception have been awakened. Why should we study spiritual teachings, the discovery of which is beyond our present scope? But the thing works rather the other way. The contemplation of the wisdom-contents which we shall perceive ever more directly with the development of our spiritual powers, is among the living forces tending to their development. The wonder and reverence that are evoked in the study of these sublime truths, the effort of clear thought that is needed, the detachment from the inevitable trivialities of outer life, the experiences one undergoes when the coherence of the Divine plan dawns upon one, and one is able to recognize in its light so many items in the life around one, transfiguring the latter, imbuing it with

18

light and inner meaning—all this is nourishment to the soul. Above all, when combined with regular meditative practice, it quickens the unfolding of the human spirit. Study, said Rudolf Steiner on one occasion, prepares the fertile ground in which the living seed of meditation is planted.

There is another reason why the study of Spiritual Science is important. All human evolution is involved— in the 20th century there is surely little need to insist on this—in the vast tragedy which is described in the religions as the Fall of Man. That the spiritual world, his true origin and home, is not generally perceptible to man in his present state, that between the material surface of things and the true reality there is a Threshold impassable to begin with and not lightly to be passed under any circumstances, this too has its inner reason. The Threshold is sternly guarded; it is indeed close to the gateway of death itself; hence, as expressed in many ceremonies and forms of ritual, ultimate Initiation always involves a coming face-to-face with death. And there is not only death itself; there are the powers of hindrance and confusion—what manifests itself in our human world as downright evil—which every human being has to meet and meet again on many levels, before he can finally receive, to use the figurative language of the Apocalypse, the crown of victory that is reserved for "him that overcometh". Precisely therefore in resolving to walk along the Path of Knowledge, to take responsibility for our life and live it henceforth out of a deeper spiritual initiative, we also challenge the great conflicts that are latent in our own as in all human life. Our hidden faults will tend to come to the surface. We shall have to face dark moments. Now a knowledge already gained by quiet open-minded study of the great facts of human evolution helps to sustain the individual when these moments come. He has the proper context in which to place his own particular trials; he will not so easily despair of himself, realizing as he will that he too is sharing in the common lot of mankind and playing his part, even through tragedy and failing, so long as his eyes are set upon the goal which is the goal of all mankind together. Here Spiritual Science sheds its light on the great Christian concepts of the redemption, the "forgiveness", the mutual bearing of burdens, the ultimate oneness of mankind.

There is, moreover, a certain danger when paths of spiritual or mental self-development are pursued, as they sometimes are, without reference to the more cosmic background that tells of mankind's evolution as a whole. The development of memory, of powers of mental concentration and the like can also lead to a narrowing, a pin-pointing of one's life and aims towards relative and temporary ends, a mere enhancement of the quest of power, if not for oneself alone, for the sectional group to which one may belong. If, on the other hand, the path is pursued in the light of a

20

universal Science, the soul will grow not only in strength but in true gentleness, imbued increasingly with a Wisdom which in its very nature is unselfish and therefore fruitful, quickening the life that is around one, recognizing and therefore serving the all-human ends even amid each limited and special task.

*   *   *

The present volume contains a selection of verses, proverbs and meditative sayings given by Rudolf Steiner during the long period of his work as spiritual teacher. Save in the sense that every expression of a deeper truth can be experienced in a meditative way, not all of them are Meditations in the proper sense. For we have also included dedications, written perhaps in a book given to a friend, or in a guest-book, and verses written for special occasions. Then there are poems and epigrammatic sayings into which Dr. Steiner cast the truths that came to him from time to time, to the elaboration of which several lectures were sometimes devoted. Indeed the lectures themselves are often material for meditation; of some of them this is true in a very special sense. We may mention for example the pictures of the creative deeds of the Hierarchies in the lecture-course *The Inner Realities of Evolution*, or the description of the ancient Mysteries collected in the volume *Mystery Centres*. Some of the verses here included were actually given at the conclusion of a lecture, summing up its contents. The date and source of the verse will generally be found in the Index, which is intended to give guidance, referring as it often does to the lecture or lecture-course in which further explanation will be found. Most of these have been published; others are available in the anthroposophical libraries in different countries. The student is strongly recommended to make use of these indications. Within the scope of this volume, only the necessary references have been given, save in a few instances where a historical or explanatory note was felt to be needed. (See the "Notes and References" at the end.)

It will be evident which of the following verses are most suitable to be chosen for regular morning and evening meditation. It will be seen that some were actually given for this purpose; through the kind help of friends, we have been able to include them. It is thus hoped that the volume will help answer a need that is often felt by those who read *Knowledge of the Higher Worlds* and wish to put into practice what is there suggested. Other collections of meditative sayings and advice by Dr. Steiner are in existence; we have referred to these in the Bibliography.

The present volume is divided into two parts. Verses suitable for meditation will be found in both; indeed, some of the deepest and most esoteric sayings are in Part I. Here too the verses are included which relate to the Festivals of the year and to the rhythms of summer and winter. Meditations specifically given by

22

Rudolf Steiner to individual pupils for morning and evening use will be found in Part II, which also contains verses for the remembrance of the dead, and others given to meet special exigencies, as mentioned on page 28.

In the early years of the present century, when working still within the framework of the Theosophical Society, Rudolf Steiner gave instruction "for those more advanced in anthroposophical spiritual knowledge" in an esoteric school, the circumstances of which are described in his Autobiography (*The Course of my Life*, Chapter XXXII). Some of the meditations and instructions given in this school were printed after his death for members of the Anthroposophical Society. In Part II we have also been able to include a few of these; they are mentioned as such in the Index.

Concerning the form of the meditations, and of meditation generally, the following should also be said. (It will be found in fuller detail in some of the works here cited.) The content of a meditation is generally given in a form of words. This, if communicated directly from the spiritual world, has a "mantric" character. There is virtue in the very sound—the rhythm of the lines, the vowels and alliterations, the repetitions. In meditation we live in the actual sound of the words, not only in their meaning. Meditation is not an intellectual reflection; we may reflect at other times on the meaning of a chosen saying. During the actual minutes of meditation we live in it in a far more quiet and receptive way.

The verses given by Rudolf Steiner—the great majority at least—were in his own tongue. In translating them it is not easy to preserve the original beauty of the form, let alone the mantric character. (More will be said concerning this at the end—see page 29.) Side by side with the translation, the original is also given. Experience has shown that very many people, even those who would not attempt to learn German for external use, acquire a sufficient knowledge of it to understand it spiritually and use it in meditation. For many people, therefore, the translation will be a bridge, leading in course of time to the direct use of the original.

That a language other than one's own can play an essential part in the inner life, has been a feature in the spiritual history of mankind throughout the ages. One thinks for instance of the part played in Christendom by Hebrew, Greek and Latin, or in the Eastern civilizations by Sanscrit. Where spiritual life prevails, man gains the power to transcend the nemesis of Babel; he enters the realm of the Logos, the Word that was in the Beginning, in which the differences are almost magically overcome. Rudolf Steiner himself also gave mantric words or sayings occasionally in Latin, Greek or Hebrew, and more especially in Sanscrit.

So much for the actual words of the meditation. But

24

the meditative life can also be a dwelling in mental pictures; indeed at a certain stage it must be so. Vivid imaginative pictures should be formed. What is here said applies not only to meditation as such; along the spiritual pathway we overcome the abstract and picture-less word-mindedness which is so prevalent in our time; we become more aware of the imaginative origin and value of the words we use.

Sometimes the meditation itself is a picture rather than a form of words. A classic example, showing how the picture is led up to in a sincere and independent-minded way, taking our start from the experiences of human life, is the Rose-Cross meditation as explained by Dr. Steiner in *An Outline of Occult Science*, Chapter V (pages 285–290 or 202–205 in the current English editions). In other instances, while imparting the words of the meditation, he would explain the picture which should be formed during or even before the inner speaking of the words. For example, with the morning meditation on page 181 he gave the following instruction: "Try to imagine the content of these lines as vividly and pictorially as you can. At the first two lines you think of an ocean of light, with spiritual forms moving in the light—formed out of the light itself. With the third, fourth and fifth lines you imagine how, on awakening, the human soul emerges from this sea of light. And at the last two lines you picture to yourself how at the moment of awakening the soul is entering again into the garments or vehicles of outer bodily existence."

Other examples of picture-meditation will be found in the "seven Seals", published with Rudolf Steiner's explanation in the collection: *Occult Seals and Columns* (cf. Note 4, page 227, and the verses on page 153). The lecture-courses mentioned on page 21 abound with imaginative pictures intended for meditation. Also in many of the lectures in which the verses in the present volume were imparted, the appropriate pictures will be found. (This applies, for example, to the sayings on page 207.)

In some of the meditations, the words are to be meditated not as if speaking them to oneself but rather hearkening—hearing them sound out of the midst of the cosmic picture or the spiritual scene that has been imagined.

When the inner mood of silence and reverence has been reached through the meditation—when, as it were, the meditation culminates—it should deliberately be ended in complete silence: no longer thinking the words or imagining the meditative picture but with the mind awake and poised, dwelling only in the inner mood and feeling which has been evoked. Often when Dr. Steiner gave to an individual pupil a morning and evening meditation in his own handwriting, it concluded with the instruction *"Ruhe bei leerem Bewusstsein"*, meaning a short period of active rest and inner silence with

26

consciousness awake, yet emptied of all content. When this arose out of the content of the meditation, Dr. Steiner often indicated the mood of the concluding silence with such words as "Christ in me", and he would specifically say: These words are put down, not to be meditated as such, but as expressing the inner feeling that will fill the concluding silence if the meditation has been rightly done.

Finally, it is important that the time devoted to meditation should be brought to an end deliberately. The meditative life is an expansion of the soul; it leads, indeed, quite literally to an expansion of what is called the "etheric body". The serene feeling which it can lead to is an expression of this. The expansion is good; but at the end we ourselves must come in again, gathering our forces for the return to the tasks of earthly life; we should never end a meditation accidentally or "at a loose end". To take a trivial but very real example: If the telephone bell should ring while we are meditating and we are obliged to answer, we should—if only for an instant—concentrate in silence, saying to ourselves with inner reverence for its content: "The meditation is ended now", and then go and do what we have to do. The traditional "Amen, so be it" of Christian prayer, or the concluding words spoken by the priest in the ritual of the Christian Community as he leaves the altar, have something of this quality. The same thing is expressed by Rudolf Steiner (see page 111) in one of his

27

Mystery Plays, at the conclusion of an instruction for meditation—an instruction of which the words are themselves a meditation:

> Yet tarry not in Worlds afar
> In dreamy play of thought.
> Begin in the vast reaches of the Spirit,
> And end in thine own Being's depths.
> There wilt thou find
> Eternal aims of Gods,
> Knowing thyself in thee.

Once more it should be emphasized that fuller explanations of the meditative path and of the whole way of knowledge will be found in Rudolf Steiner's books, notably those given in the Bibliography on page 239.

This book also contains a number of verses and meditations for special occasions. Given to meet an individual need, or the circumstances of the time, these are obviously of universal value. Among them are the meditative prayers for use during illness; also the verses given at the time of the War (1914–18); and above all, the meditations recommended for sending one's thoughts towards the dead. Notably during the War, when so many people were being separated by violent and sudden death from those near and dear to them, Dr. Steiner indicated how the connection with souls who have gone on into the spiritual world can be cultivated —for their sakes as well as for the sake of mankind on Earth. How the remembrance of the dead in this realistic

28

sense will become part of spiritual culture ever more and more, was shown by Dr. Steiner in many different connections. Here again we have indicated in the Bibliography lectures and writings in which the use of such meditations for the dead, and other cognate matters, are explained in detail.

*   *   *

Concerning the Translations

The translations in this volume, save in the few instances here mentioned, are by George and Mary Adams. The verses given at Easter 1924 (pages 75 and 77) were translated by Mrs. E. Bowen-Wedgwood; the Christmas Poem "Behold the Sun at the Midnight Hour" (page 71) by Frances Melland; and the verse for the opening of Group Meetings (page 195) and also the verses on page 205 by Mrs. E. R. Cull. "Grace before Meals" (page 41) is by an unknown translator.

Many of the verses and meditative sayings have been published in different translations in the Lectures, Mystery Plays or other works where they occur. These are mentioned in the Index.

Translation obviously cannot be literal. We have some knowledge of Rudolf Steiner's occasional comments and advice on this matter. He looked for an adequate rendering—in the genius of the other language—of the idea or picture or line of thought, taken as a whole. Often he would point out that the obvious dictionary translation of a word can in a deeper sense be quite untrue; the examples he gave show how far afield he himself felt it right to go. In the translations here given, we have not attempted a word-for-word correspondence, but have tried to be true to the spirit and integral effect of the original.

Translations of this kind must therefore be an individual responsibility. With the original on the opposite page, it will be only too easy to ascertain that such and such a word does not correspond and to replace it by a more literal rendering. When this is done, it throws out of balance what has been conceived as a whole, and will rarely, if ever, be an improvement. Those who have sincerely grappled with the inherent difficulties will be the first to admit that better renderings may be made than their own. But these should then be done entirely afresh from the original. It is therefore requested that the translations here given be not altered without consultation.

A number of verses will here be found containing the name of the Archangel Michael. Rudolf Steiner was insistent that when this name refers to a Divine Being it should be pronounced Micha-el, with the three syllables fully articulate and distinct. He did not criticize the usual pronunciation when the name is used as a "Christian name" in human intercourse; also he took it for granted that the vowel and consonant sounds would be pronounced as is customary in our language. But the concluding syllable EL, he said, being the Name of God, should on no account be slurred over when speaking of a Hierarchical Being.

It will be noted that in the English of these verses the full three syllables of the name Micha-el have been allowed for. The rhythm and effect of the verse will be marred if it is not spoken in this way.

Our selection has partly been determined by the relative possibility of translation. Many of Rudolf Steiner's most beautiful and valuable verses are not included for the simple reason that an adequate translation seemed beyond our powers. With the spread and deepening of the spiritual movement initiated by this great Western teacher, it may be hoped that future translators will succeed where we have failed.

*   *   *

The initiative for this publication is largely due to the Council of the Anthroposophical Society in Great Britain, who have also participated in the final form of this Introduction; we are grateful for many valuable suggestions.

Finally, our thanks are due to the *Rudolf Steiner Nachlassverwaltung* for their encouragement and collaboration in the compiling of this volume, and for kindly allowing us to include several items which are here published for the first time not only in translation, but in the original.

Part I

Warum strebt des Menschen
Suchende Seele
Nach Erkenntnis
Der höheren Welten?
Weil jeder seeleentsprossene Blick
In die Sinneswelt
Zur sehnsuchtsvollen Frage wird
Nach dem Geistessein.

Why does the seeking soul of Man
Strive towards knowledge of higher Worlds?
Because every look—born of the soul—
Into the outer world of Nature
Turns to the question, fraught with longing:
Where is the Being Divine?

Wie die Blüt' und Frucht,
Vom Sonnengeist gereift,
Sich dem Pflanzenstamm entringt;
So entsteigt der Wahrheit Lichtesblüte
Dem Seelenstamm des Menschen,
Vom Göttlich = Guten wohlgepflegt.
Drüm strebt nach Wahrheit
Ein jeder gute Mensch,
Gleichwie zum Lichte
Die Pflanze streben müss;
Will sie vor dem Blühen nicht verdorren.

36

Even as blossom and fruit,
By the Sun-Spirit ripened,
Spring from the flowering stem,
So from the stem of man's inner being
Will Truth uplift his budding cup of light,
Tended by God and nurtured by the Good.
Therefore to the Truth
Every good man aspires,
As to the Light
The plant reaches out
Lest it droop ere it come to flower.

Der Sonne Licht,
Es hellt den Tag
Nach finstrer Nacht.
Der Seele Kraft,
Sie ist erwacht
Aus Schlafes Ruh':
Du meine Seele,
Sei dankbar dem Licht,
Es leuchtet in ihm
Des Gottes Macht;
Du meine Seele,
Sei tüchtig zur Tat.

The Light of the Sun
Brightens all Space
When dark night is past.
The life of the soul
Now is awakened
From restful Sleep.
O thou, my soul,
Give thanks to the Light.
In it shines forth
The Power of God.
O thou, my soul,
Be strong for deeds.

TISCHGEBET

Es keimen die Pflanzen in der Erdennacht,
Es sprossen die Kräuter durch der Luft Gewalt,
Es reifen die Früchte durch der Sonne Macht.

So keimet die Seele in des Herzens Schrein,
So sprosset des Geistes Macht im Licht der Welt,
So reifet des Menschen Kraft in Gottes Schein.

GRACE BEFORE MEALS

The plant-seeds are quickened in the night of the Earth,
The green herbs are sprouting through the might of the Air,
And all fruits are ripened by the power of the Sun.

So quickens the soul in the shrine of the Heart,
So blossoms Spirit-power in the light of the World,
So ripens Man's strength in the glory of God.

Im Herzen
Lebt ein Menschenglied,
Das von allen
Stoff enthält,
Der am meisten geistig ist;
Das von allen
Geistig lebt
In der Art, die am meisten
Stofflich sich offenbart.

Daher ist Sonne
Im Menschen-Weltall
Das Herz;
Daher ist im Herzen
Der Mensch
Am meisten
In seines Wesens
Tiefstem Quell.

In the human Heart
there lives a part of Man
which contains matter
more spiritual than in any other organ;
also a part of Man
of which the spiritual life
is made more manifest in matter
than that of any other organ.

Hence in the Microcosm that is Man
Sun is the Heart,
and in his Heart is Man united
most of all with the deepest fount—
the fount of his true Being.

Im Kopfe Glaubenskraft,
Im Herzen Liebensmacht,
Im vollen Menschen starkes Hoffen
Hält und trägt das Leben.

In the Head the power of Faith,
In the Heart the might of Love,
In the full human being all-sustaining Hope.

Im freien Menschenwesen
Fasset das Weltall sich zusammen.
Darum fasse dich mit freiem Sinne
Und du findest die Welt
Und durch dich wird der Geist der Welt.

In the free being of Man
The Universe is gathered up.
Then in the free resolve of your heart
Take your own life in hand,
And you will find the World.
The Spirit of the World will find itself in you.

Im grenzenlosen Aussen
Finde dich als Menschenwesen.

Im engsten Innenleben
Fühle Welten unbegrenzt.

So wird es sich enthüllen,
Dass der Weltenrätsel Lösung
Der Mensch nur selber ist.

In the boundless Without
Find thyself, oh Man!

In the innermost Within
Feel the boundless Worlds!

So will it be revealed:
Nowhere the Riddle of Worlds is solved,
Save in the being of Man.

Wenn du auf den Geist des Weltenseins
Dein Augenmerk zu lenken dich bemühst,
So wirst du dich selber finden
Als freier Mensch im Schicksalsfelde.

Wenn du dich abwendest von ihm
Und nur auf des Tages Scheineswesen
Den Sinn gerichtet halten wirst,
So wirst du dich verlieren
Als Menschenbild im Schicksalsspiele.

If to the Spirit of the All-World Being
Thou turn with heart and mind,
Then wilt thou find thyself:
Free man and sovereign player
In the fields of Fate.

But if thou turn from Him away
And in vain glory of the hour find distraction,
Then wilt thou lose thyself:
Tossed like the empty figment of a man,
The toy of Fate.

Was habt ihr Truggedanken, Blendgesichter,
Zu tun mit Hohem, das ich soll;
Die Geister wollen's doch von mir.
So schaff' ich der eignen Seele Feindschaft
Mich zwingend zu kräft'gem Denken
Mir aus dem zagenden Herzen,
Das stark mir dient, will ich es nur.

SHIRKING RESPONSIBILITY

Vain fancyings and figments of illusion,
What have you to do
With the high purpose that is set before me?
The spiritual Beings want it of me.
Then will I be my own soul's adversary,
And summon up this vacillating heart
To clear and honest thinking—
The heart that serves me, strong and true,
If I but will it so.

Der eigenen Seele Geheimnisse
Ergründe in dem Antlitz,
Das die Welt dir zuwendet.
Der Welten Innensein
Ergründe in dem Antlitz,
Das sie deiner Seele prägt.

Perceive the secrets of thy soul
In the countenance
The wide world turns towards thee.
Perceive the living essence of the World
In the countenance
Imprinted by it on thine inmost soul.

Es lassen die Elemente
Gestaltend sich vom Geist durchdringen.
Empfangen mussten sie
Des Geistes letzten Kräftetrieb,
Das Menschenwesen einzukleiden
In Geistgestalt und Seelenleben.

The Elements allow the Spirit
To form them through and through.
And they received the last and deepest
Informing of the Spirit,
That they might clothe the being of Man
With life of soul and spiritual stature.

Im Weltenall
Webet des Menschen Wesenheit.
Im Menschenkern
Waltet der Welten Spiegelbild.

Das Ich verbindet beide
Und schaffet so
Des Daseins wahren Sinn.

Through the wide world there lives and moves
The real Being of Man,
While in the innermost core of Man
The mirror-image of the World is living.

The I unites the two,
And thus fulfils
The meaning of existence.

Die Welt im Ich erbauen,
Das Ich in Welten schauen
Ist Seelenatem.

Erleben des All
In Selbst-Erfühlung
Ist Weisheitpuls.

Und Wege des Geistes
Im eignen Ziel beschreiben
Ist Wahrheitsprache.

Und Seelenatem dringe
In Weisheitpuls, erlösend
Aus Menschengründen
Die Wahrheitsprache
In Lebens-Jahres-Rhythmen.

To build the World in the I ,
To behold the I in the World,
Is breathing of the soul.

To sense the Universal All
In feeling of one's inner self
Is Wisdom's pulse.

To trace the paths of the Spirit
In one's own aims of life
Is inner speech of Truth.

So let the soul's breath penetrate
Into the pulse of Wisdom, calling forth
From inmost depths
The speech of Truth
Through all the rhythms of the years of life.

Es wechseln in des Jahres Lauf
Des Sommers Wachstumskraft
Und Winters Erdenruh'.
Und in des Menschen Lebensbahn
Auch wechselt Wachens Kraft
Mit Schlafens Friedewalten;
Doch lebt im Schlaf' und Wachen
Die geisterfüllte Seele fort.
So auch lebt die Erdenseele geistig
Im Sommers- und im Winters-Wandel.

In the year's course
Alternate ceaselessly
Summer's abounding growth
And Winter's Earth-repose;
So in the course of Man's life
Vigour of waking day
And peaceful bounty of sleep.
Yet does the Spirit-filled soul live on—
Sleeping and waking.
So in the Spirit, the soul of the Earth
Lives through the seasons' changing—
Summer and Winter.

SONNENWENDE

Es schläft der Erde Seele
In Sommers heisser Zeit;
Da strahlet helle
Der Sonne Spiegel
Im äusseren Raum.

Es wacht der Erde Seele
In Winters kalter Zeit;
Da leuchtet geistig
Die wahre Sonne
Im innern Sein.

Sommers-Freude-Tag
Ist Erden-Schlaf;
Winter-Weihe-Nacht
Ist Erden-Tag.

Summer and Winter

Asleep is the soul of Earth
In Summer's heat,
While the Sun's outward Glory
Rays through the realms of Space.

Awake is the soul of Earth
In Winter's cold,
While the Sun's inmost Being
Lightens in Spirit.

Summer's day of joy
For Earth is sleep.
Winter's holy night
For Earth is day.

WEIHNACHT

Im Seelenaug' sich spiegelt
Der Erde Hoffnungslicht,
Der Welten heil'ge Weisheit
Zu Menschenherzen spricht:
Des Vaters ewige Liebe
Den Sohn zur Erde sendet,
Der gnadevoll dem Menschenpfade
Die Himmelshelle spendet.

CHRISTMAS

In the eye of the soul is mirrored
The light of hope of the Earth.
Holy Wisdom of Worlds
Speaks in the heart of Man:
The Father's eternal Love
Sends to the Earth the Son,
Who on Man's pathway sheds
Bounty of Heaven's Light.

WEIHNACHT

In des Menschen Seelengründen
Lebt die Geistes-Sonne siegessicher.
Des Gemütes rechte Kräfte,
Sie vermögen sie zu ahnen
In des Innern Winterleben;
Und des Herzens Hoffnungstrieb,
Er erschaut den Sonnen-Geistes-Sieg
In dem Weihnacht-Segenslichte,
Als dem Sinnbild höchsten Lebens
In des Winters tiefer Nacht.

CHRISTMAS

Deep in the ground of the human soul,
Of victory assured,
The Spirit-Sun is living.
All through the winter of the inner life
The faithful heart divines it.
Now the heart's spring of hope beholds
The Sun, His coming glory
In Christmas' light of blessing—
Token of highest life
In winter's deepest night.

Die Sonne schaue
Um mitternächtige Stunde.
Mit Steinen baue
Im leblosen Grunde.

So finde im Niedergang
Und in des Todes Nacht
Der Schöpfung neuen Anfang,
Des Morgens junge Macht.

Die Höhen lass offenbaren
Der Götter ewiges Wort;
Die Tiefen sollen bewahren
Den friedevollen Hort.

Im Dunkel lebend
Erschaffe eine Sonne.
Im Stoffe webend
Erkenne Geistes Wonne.

Winter Solstice

Behold the Sun
At the midnight hour!
In the lifeless ground
Build thy rocky bower!

So, when in depths thou mourn,
Find thou in Death's dark night
Creation's pulse new-born
With living Morning Light.

The Powers on high make known
The eternal Word Divine;
The Deeps must guard their own—
Peace, in their sacred shrine.

In gloom thou livest—
Create anew a Sun!
In matter weavest—
Know Spirit-bliss begun!

WEIHNACHT

Des irdischen Menschheitwerdens
Sonnen-Aufgang,
Das ist das Geheimnis
Auf dem Golgatha-Berg;
Im Weihnacht-Licht
Erstrahlet die Morgendämmerung.
In dieser Dämmerung
Mildem Licht
Verehr' die Seele
Des eignen Wesens
Geistverwandte
Daseinsmacht und Quelle.

CHRISTMAS

Sunrise of mankind's earthly pilgrimage—
Such is the secret
On the hill of Golgotha.
Kindled on Christmas night
Is the first heralding of dawn.
Now in this dawning's
Gentle light
The soul shall contemplate
Her own true Being's
Spirit-kindred
Living force and fount.

OSTERN

Steh' vor des Menschen Lebenspforte:
Schau' an ihrer Stirne Weltenworte.

Leb' in des Menschen Seeleninnern:
Fühl' in seinem Kreise Weltbeginnen.

Denk' an des Menschen Erdenende:
Find' bei ihm die Geisteswende.

EASTER

Stand in the porch at Man's life-entrance,
Read thereon the World's writ sentence.

Dwell in the soul of Man within,
Feel, in its pulsing, Worlds begin.

Think upon Man's earthly ending,
Find therein the Spirit's wending.

OSTERN

Das Mysterium zu Ephesus

Weltentsprossenes Wesen, du in Lichtgestalt,
Von der Sonne erkraftet in der Mondgewalt,

Dich beschenket des Mars erschaffendes Klingen
Und Merkurs gliedbewegendes Schwingen,

Dich erleuchtet Jupiters erstrahlende Weisheit
Und der Venus liebetragende Schönheit —

Dass Saturns weltenalte Geist-Innigkeit
Dich dem Raumessein und Zeitenwerden weihe!

EASTER

The Mystery of Ephesus

Offspring of all the Worlds! Thou in a form of light,
Firm framèd by the Sun, with Luna's might,

Endowed with sounding Mars' life-stirring hymns,
And swift-winged Mercury's motion in thy limbs,

Illum'd with royal Jupiter's all-wiseness,
And grace-bestowing Venus' loveliness—

That ghostly Saturn's old-world-memoried devoutness
Unto the world of Space and Time thee hallow!

Rätsel an Rätsel stellt sich im Raum,
Rätsel an Rätsel läuft in der Zeit;
Lösung bringt der Geist nur,
Der sich ergreift
Jenseits von Raumesgrenzen und
Jenseits vom Zeitenlauf.

Riddles untold in the widths of Space,
Riddles untold in the rounds of Time!
Only the wakened Spirit can solve them, holding its own
Beyond the confines of Space, beyond the flow of Time.

PFINGSTEN

Wo Sinneswissen endet,
Da stehet erst die Pforte,
Die Lebenswirklichkeiten
Dem Seelensein eröffnet.
Den Schlüssel schafft die Seele,
Wenn sie in sich erstarket
Im Kampf, den Weltenmächte
Auf ihrem eignen Grunde
Mit Menschenkräften führen;
Wenn sie durch sich vertreibt
Den Schlaf, der Wissenskräfte
An ihren Sinnesgrenzen
Mit Geistesnacht umhüllet.

WHITSUNTIDE

Where outer senses' knowledge ends,
There and there only is the gateway
That leads to the realities of life.
The soul of Man himself forges the key
When he grows strong in the battle
Which cosmic powers with human powers wage
Upon the soul's deep ground,
And by his own free will dispels the sleep
Which at the senses' frontiers
Plunges in spiritual night
His faculties of knowledge.

PFINGST-STIMMUNG

Wesen reiht sich an Wesen in Raumesweiten,
Wesen folgt auf Wesen in Zeitenläufen.
Verbleibst du in Raumesweiten, in Zeitenläufen,
So bist du, o Mensch, im Reiche der Vergänglichkeiten.
Über sie aber erhebt deine Seele sich gewaltiglich,
Wenn sie ahnend oder wissend schaut das Unvergängliche,
Jenseits der Raumesweiten, jenseits der Zeitenläufe.

82

PENTECOST

Creature ranks with creature in the widths of Space,
Creature follows creature in the rounds of Time.
Linger, oh Man, in widths of Space, in rounds of Time,—
You are in realms that fade and pass away.
Yet mightily your soul rises above them
When you divine or knowingly behold the Eternal
Beyond the confines of Space, beyond the flow of Time.

Wir Menschen der Gegenwart
Brauchen das rechte Gehör
Für des Geistes Morgenruf,
Den Morgenruf des Michael.
Geist-Erkenntnis will
Der Seele erschliessen
Dies wahre Morgenruf-Hören.

We men of present time
Need to give ear to the Spirit's morning call—
The call of Micha-el.
Spiritual Knowledge seeks
To open in the soul of man
True hearing of this morning call.

Ringende Geisteskräfte
Streben im Stoff;
Sie finden nicht den Stoff,
Sie finden sich selber.
Sie schweben über Natürlichem,
Sie leben in sich selber:
Michael-Kraft atmend.

Powers of the Spirit, powers of thought
Wrestle with matter.
It is not matter they find,—
They find themselves.
They hover over the natural life,
Living within themselves,
Breathing the bounty of Micha-el.

Waltender, weiser Willensgeist,
Webend in Geistesweiten allüberall,
Wirkend durch Geisteswesenheiten—
Wirkest sicher du
In meinen Seelenwesenstiefen auch.
So binde liebewirkend stark
Mein Inneres an deine lichte Kraft.
Dich findend, find ich mich.

88

Wisdom-wielding Spirit of Will,
Weaving the Spirit-Worlds throughout,
Working through Spirit-Beings,
Working in the depths of my being too:
Weld with the fire of thy Love
My inner being with thy light and strength,
That finding thee I may find myself.

MICHAELS SCHWERT
Meteorisches Eisen

O Mensch,
Du bildest es zu deinem Dienste,
Du offenbarst es seinem Stoffeswerte nach
In vielen deiner Werke.
Es wird dir Heil jedoch erst sein,
Wenn dir sich offenbart
Seines Geistes Hochgewalt.

SWORD OF MICHA-EL
Iron and Meteoric Iron

O Man,
Thou mouldest it to thy service.
In its material value thou revealest it
In many of thy works.
Yet it will only bring thee Healing
When to thee is revealed
The Power sublime of its indwelling Spirit.

MICHAEL-IMAGINATION

Sonnenmächten Entsprossene,
Leuchtende, Welten begnadende
Geistesmächte, zu Michaels Strahlenkleid
Seid ihr vorbestimmt vom Götterdenken.

Er, der Christusbote, weist in euch
Menschentragenden, heil'gen Welten-Willen;
Ihr, die hellen Aetherwelten-Wesen,
Trägt das Christuswort zum Menschen.

So erscheint der Christuskünder
Den erharrenden, durstenden Seelen;
Ihnen strahlet euer Leuchte-Wort
In des Geistesmenschen Weltenzeit.

Ihr, der Geist-Erkenntnis Schüler,
Nehmet Michaels weises Winken,
Nehmt des Welten-Willens Liebe-Wort
In der Seelen Höhenziele wirksam auf.

MICHAEL IMAGINATION

Springing from Powers of the Sun,
Radiant Spirit-powers, blessing all Worlds!
For Micha-el's garment of rays
Ye are predestinèd by Thought Divine.

He, the Christ-messenger, revealeth in you—
Bearing mankind aloft—the sacred Will of Worlds.
Ye, the radiant Beings of Aether-Worlds,
Bear the Christ-Word to Man.

Thus shall the Herald of Christ appear
To the thirstily waiting souls,
To whom your Word of Light shines forth
In cosmic age of Spirit-Man.

Ye, the disciples of Spirit-Knowledge,
Take Micha-el's Wisdom beckoning,
Take the Word of Love of the Will of Worlds
Into your souls' aspiring, actively!

Die Empfindung des Menschen der dritten Kulturperiode

O, dunkel ist der Erde Antlitz,
Wenn die Sonne blendend dunkelt.
Doch hell wird mir mein Tagefeld,
Wenn die Seele es beleuchtet
Durch Sternenweisheit.

Dark is the face of Earth
When darkened by the Sun's blinding ray.
But light and clear becomes my day's horizon
When the soul's inner life illumines it
With Wisdom from the Stars.

Sterne sprachen einst zu Menschen,
Ihr Verstummen ist Weltenschicksal;
Des Verstummens Wahrnehmung
Kann Leid sein des Erdenmenschen;

In der stummen Stille aber reift
Was Menschen sprechen zu Sternen;
Ihres Sprechens Wahrnehmung
Kann Kraft werden des Geistesmenschen.

The Stars spake once to Man.
It is World-destiny
That they are silent now.
To be aware of the silence
Can become pain for earthly Man.

But in the deepening silence
There grows and ripens
What Man speaks to the Stars.
To be aware of the speaking
Can become strength for Spirit-Man.

Es keimen die Pflanzen im Erdengrund,
Es strömen die Regen aus Himmelshöhen;
Es keimt die Liebe im Menschenherzen,
Es strömt die Weisheit in Menschengeister.

The plant-seeds spring in the womb of Earth
And Waters rain from Heaven's heights.
So does Love spring in human hearts
And Wisdom water the thoughts of men.

In der Lichtesluft des Geisterlandes
Da erblüh'n die Seelenrosen,
Und ihr Rot erstrahlet
In die Erdenschwere;
Es wird im Menschenwesen
Zum Herzgebild verdichtet:
Es strahlet in der Bluteskraft
Als das Erdenrosenrot
In die Geistesfelder wieder hin.

In Light-and-Air of Spirit-Land
There grow the roses of the soul.
And their raying red, downpouring
Into the weight of Earth
Fashions the heart of Man.
It rays again in the force of blood—
The rose-red of the Earth —
Forth into the Spirit-fields.

Im Farbenschein des Äthermeeres
Gebiert des Lichtes webend Wesen
Der Menschenseele Geistgewebe;
Und geistbefruchtet reifend strebt
In Farbendunkels Raumestiefe
Hinaus die Lichtes-durst'ge Seele.
Bedürftig ist Natur des Geistes,
Der aus dem Seelensein ihr kraftet;
Bedürftig auch die Menschenseele
Der Kraft des Lichts im Weltenäther.

In the ethereal ocean's colour-glorying
The weaving essence of the Light brings forth
The Spirit-texture of the Soul of Man,
And ripening with seed of Spirit-life
The Soul athirst for Light looks out
Into the darkling colour-depths of Space.

Nature hath need of the Spirit
Which from the Soul's inner life wells forth to meet her.
So too the human Soul hath need
Of the abounding Light in the World-ether-sea.

In dem Herzen webet Fühlen,
In dem Haupte leuchtet Denken,
In den Gliedern kraftet Wollen.
Webendes Leuchten,
Kraftendes Weben,
Leuchtendes Kraften:
Das ist der Mensch.

In the Heart—the loom of Feeling,
In the Head—the light of Thinking,
In the Limbs—the strength of Will.
Weaving of radiant Light,
Strength of the Weaving,
Light of the surging Strength:
Lo, this is Man!

Du selbst, erkennender, fühlender, wollender Mensch,
Du bist das Rätsel der Welt.
Was sie verbirgt,
In dir wird es offenbar, es wird
In deinem Geiste Licht,
In deiner Seele Wärme,
Und deines Atems Kraft,
Sie bindet dir die Leibeswesenheit
An Seelenwelten,
An Geistesreiche.
Sie führt dich in den Stoff,
Dass du dich menschlich findest;
Sie führt dich in den Geist,
Dass du dich geistig nicht verlierest.

You, Man, yourself—knowing, feeling and willing—
You are the riddle of the World.
What in the World is concealed
Grows manifest in you.
It becomes light in your Spirit,
It becomes warmth in your soul.
Your breathing welds your body's life
To worlds of soul and realms of Spirit.
It leads you into the world of matter
That you may find your manhood,
And that you lose not yourself on the way,
It guides you into the Spirit.

Im Suchen erkenne dich,
Und wesend wirst du dir.
Entzieht das Suchen sich dir:
Du hast dich zwar im Sein,
Doch Sein entreisset dir
Des eignen Wesens Wahrheit.

In seeking know thyself,—
So shalt thou become thy being.
But if thou cease from seeking,—
Whate'er thou hast, whate'er thou art,
This will itself take away from thee
True being of thy being.

In deinem Denken leben Weltgedanken,
In deinem Fühlen weben Weltenkräfte,
In deinem Willen wirken Weltenwesen.
Verliere dich in Weltgedanken,
Erlebe dich durch Weltenkräfte
Erschaffe dich aus Willenswesen.
Bei Weltenfernen ende nicht
Durch Denkentraumesspiel—;
Beginne in den Geistesweiten,
Und ende in den eignen Seelentiefen:—
Du findest Götterziele
Erkennend dich in dir.

In thy thinking World-wide Thoughts are living,
In thy Feeling World-All Forces weaving,
In thy Willing World-Beings working.
Lose thyself in World-wide Thoughts,
Feel thyself through World-All Forces,
Create thyself from Beings of Will.
Yet tarry not in Worlds afar
In dreamy play of thought.
Begin in the vast reaches of the Spirit,
And end in thine own Being's depths.
There wilt thou find
Eternal aims of Gods,
Knowing thyself in thee.

Es keimen der Seele Wünsche,
Es wachsen des Willens Taten,
Es reifen des Lebens Früchte.

Ich fühle mein Schicksal,
Mein Schicksal findet mich.
Ich fühle meinen Stern,
Mein Stern findet mich.
Ich fühle meine Ziele,
Meine Ziele finden mich.

Meine Seele und die Welt sind Eines nur.

Das Leben, es wird heller um mich,
Das Leben, es wird schwerer für mich,
Das Leben, es wird reicher in mir.

The wishes of the soul are springing,
The deeds of the will are thriving,
The fruits of life are maturing.

I feel my fate,
My fate finds me.
I feel my star,
My star finds me.
I feel my goals in life,
My goals in life are finding me.

My soul and the great World are one.

Life grows more radiant about me,
Life grows more arduous for me,
Grows more abundant within me.

Es muss sein Sondersein und Leben opfern,
Wer Geistesziele schauen will
Durch Sinnesoffenbarung;
Wer sich erkühnen will,
In seinen Eigenwillen
Den Geisteswillen zu ergiessen.

He must be ready to forgo
His separate existence,
To sacrifice his life,
Who would behold the aims of the Eternal
In Nature's outward revelation,
And dare to pour the Spirit's will
Into his own.

Heilsam ist nur, wenn
Im Spiegel der Menschenseele
Sich bildet die ganze Gemeinschaft
Und in der Gemeinschaft
Lebet der Einzelseele Kraft.

Dies ist das Motto der Sozialethik

The healthy social life is found
when in the mirror of each human soul
the whole community finds its reflection,
and when in the community
the virtue of each one is living.

This is the Motto of Social Ethic

Der Wahrheit Same liegt in der Liebe;
Der Liebe Wurzel suche in der Wahrheit—
So spricht dein höheres Selbst.

Des Feuers Glut wandelt
Holz in wärmenden Strahl,
Des Wissens lösender Wille
Das Werk in die Kraft.

Dein Werk sei der Schatten,
Den dein Ich wirft,
Wenn es beschienen wird
Durch die Flamme
Deines höheren Selbst.

In Love lives the seed of Truth,
In Truth seek the root of Love:
Thus speaks thy higher Self.

The fire's glow transmutes
Wood into warming rays.
Wisdom's resolving Will
Changes the outer work
Into abiding strength.

So let thy work be the shadow
Cast by thine I
When it is lit by the flame—
Flame of thy higher Self.

Es wollte im Sinnenstoffe
Das Goetheanum vom Ewigen
In Formen zum Auge sprechen:
Die Flammen konnten den Stoff verzehren.
Es soll die Anthroposophie
Aus Geistigem ihren Bau
Zur Seele sprechen lassen:
Die Flammen des Geistes,
Sie werden sie erhärten.

Made out of Nature's materials,
The Goetheanum wanted to speak through its forms
Of the Eternal to the eyes of men.
The flames were able to consume the matter.
Henceforward Anthroposophia—
Her edifice formed of the Spirit—
Shall speak to the inner soul of man
In words of fire, tempered by the flames—
The flames of the Spirit.

Isis-Sophia,
Des Gottes Weisheit,
Sie hat Luzifer getötet
Und auf der Weltenkräfte Schwingen
In Raumesweiten fortgetragen.

Christus-Wollen
In Menschen wirkend,
Es wird Luzifer entreissen
Und auf des Geisteswissens Booten
In Menschenseelen auferwecken
Isis-Sophia,
Des Gottes Weisheit.

Isis-Sophia,
Wisdom of God:
Lucifer hath slain her
And on the wings of the World-wide Forces
Carried her hence into cosmic Space.

Christ-Will
Working in Man
Shall wrest from Lucifer
And on the sails of Spirit-knowledge
Call to new life in souls of men
Isis-Sophia,
Wisdom of God.

Des Lichtes webend Wesen, es erstrahlet
Durch Raumesweiten,
Zu füllen die Welt mit Sein.
Der Liebe Segen, er erwarmet
Die Zeitenfolgen,
Zu rufen aller Welten Offenbarung.
Und Geistesboten, sie vermählen
Des Lichtes webend Wesen
Mit Seelenoffenbarung;
Und wenn vermählen kann mit beiden
Der Mensch sein eigen Selbst,
Ist er in Geisteshöhen lebend.

124

FROM *The Portal of Initiation*

The weaving essence of the Light rays forth
Through realms of Space
To fill the World with Being.
Love's blessing warms the rounds of Time
To call all Worlds to their revealing.
And Angel-beings, they unite
Light's weaving essence with the Souls of Worlds.
And when Man welds with both of these
His inmost Being,
He is alive in Spirit-Heights.

Des Lichtes webend Wesen, es erstrahlet
Von Mensch zu Mensch,
Zu füllen alle Welt mit Wahrheit.
Der Liebe Segen, er erwarmet
Die Seele an der Seele,
Zu wirken aller Welten Seligkeit.
Und Geistesboten, sie vermählen
Der Menschen Segenswerke
Mit Weltenzielen;
Und wenn vermählen kann die beiden
Der Mensch, der sich im Menschen findet,
Erstrahlet Geisteslicht durch Seelenwärme.

The weaving essence of the Light rays forth
From Man to Man
To fill the World with Truth.
Love's blessing warmeth Soul by Soul,
To call forth bounty of all Worlds.
And Angel-beings, they unite
Man's deeds of blessing with World-aims Divine.
And when Man, welding both, beholds
Himself in Spirit-Man,
Then Light of Spirit rays
  through Warmth of Soul.

In der Zeiten Wende
Trat das Welten-Geistes-Licht
In den irdischen Wesensstrom;
Nacht-Dunkel
Hatte ausgewaltet;
Taghelles Licht
Erstrahlte in Menschenseelen;
Licht,
Das erwärmet
Die armen Hirtenherzen;
Licht,
Das erleuchtet
Die weisen Königshäupter.

Göttliches Licht,
Christus-Sonne,
Erwärme
Unsere Herzen,
Erleuchte
Unsere Häupter,
Dass gut werde,
Was wir
Aus Herzen gründen,
Was wir
Aus Häuptern
Zielvoll führen wollen.

At the turning-point of Time,
The Spirit-Light of the World
Entered the stream of Earthly Evolution.
Darkness of Night
Had held its sway;
Day-radiant Light
Poured into the souls of men:
Light that gave warmth
To simple shepherds' hearts,
Light that enlightened
The wise heads of kings.

O Light Divine!
O Sun of Christ!
Warm Thou our hearts,
Enlighten Thou our heads,
That good may become
What from our hearts we would found
And from our heads direct
With single purpose.

PART II

ÜBER DAS CHRISTUS-EREIGNIS

Was durch die Christus - Erscheinung der Menschheitsentwickelung zugeflossen ist, wirkte wie ein Same in derselben. Der Same kann nur allmählich reifen. Nur der allergeringste Teil der Tiefen der neuen Weistümer ist bis auf die Gegenwart herein in das physische Dasein eingeflossen. Dieses steht erst im Anfange der christlichen Entwickelung.

All that was poured into human evolution through Christ's coming, worked in it like a seed. Slowly the seed must ripen. Only a little part of the depth and content of the new Wisdom has flowed into physical existence up to the present. We are only at the beginning of Christian evolution.

Es kann gewusst werden das Mysterium des Gottesweges.
Derjenige, der sich offenbarte durch das Fleisch,
Dessen Wesen aber in sich geistig ist,
Der voll erkennbar den Engeln nur ist,
Aber doch gepredigt werden konnte den Heiden,
Der im Glauben der Welt Leben hat:
Er ist erhoben in die Sphäre der Geister der Weisheit.

134

The Mystery of the Way of God can now be known.
He who revealed Himself in and through the flesh,
Whose whole Being is yet spiritual through and through,—
He who is fully recognizable only to the Angels,
Who was yet able to be proclaimed to all peoples—
Whose very life is in the Faith of the World:
He has been lifted up into the sphere of the Spirits of Wisdom.

From I. Timothy (Chapter 3, verse 16)

135

In gegenwärtiger Erdenzeit
Braucht der Mensch erneut
Geistigen Inhalt für die Worte seiner Rede;
Denn von der Sprache
Behalten Seele und Geist
Für die Zeit des schlafenden
Weilens ausser dem Leibe
Das vom Wort, was auf Geistiges weist.
Denn es müssen schlafende Menschen
Bis zur Verständigung
Mit den Archangeloi kommen.
Die aber nehmen nur Geist-Inhalt,
Nicht Materien-Inhalt der Worte auf.
Fehlt dem Menschen diese Verständigung,
Nimmt er Schaden an seinem ganzen Wesen.

In present earthly Time
Man needs renewed spiritual content
in the words he speaks.
For of the spoken word Man's soul and spirit
during the time outside the body while he sleeps
retain whatever is of spiritual value.
For sleeping Man needs to reach out
into the realm of the Archangeloi
for conversation with them;
and they can only receive the spiritual content—
never the material content of the words.
Failing such conversation,
Man suffers harm in his entire being.

Des Geistes Sphäre ist der Seele Heimat;
Und der Mensch gelangt dahin,
Geht er den Weg des wahren Denkens,
Wählt er des Herzens Liebekraft
Zum starken Führer sich,
Und öffnet er den inneren Seelensinn
Der Schrift, die überall
Im Weltensein sich offenbaret,
Die er stets finden kann
Als Geistverkündigung
In allem, was da lebt und lebend wirkt,
In allen Dingen auch,
Die leblos sich im Raume breiten,
In allem, was geschieht
Im Werdestrom der Zeit.

The sphere of the Spirit is the soul's true home,
And Man will surely reach it
By walking in the path of honest Thought;
By choosing as his guide the fount of Love
Implanted in his heart;
By opening the eye of his soul
To Nature's script
Spread out before him through all the Universe,
Telling the story of the Spirit
In all that lives and thrives,
And in the silent spaciousness of lifeless things,
And in the stream of Time—the process of becoming.

Sieh, du mein Auge
Der Sonne reine Strahlen
Aus der Erde Formenwesen.

Sieh, du mein Herz
Der Sonne Geistgewalten
Aus des Wassers Wellenschlägen.

Sieh, du meine Seele
Der Sonne Weltenwillen
Aus der Lüfte Glanzgeflimmer.

Sieh, du mein Geist
Der Sonne Götterwesen
Aus des Feuers Liebeströmen.

See thou, mine eye,
The Sun's pure rays
In crystal forms of Earth.

See thou, my heart,
The Sun's Spirit-power
In Water's surging wave.

See thou, my soul,
The Sun's cosmic will
In quivering gleam of Air.

See thou, my Spirit,
The Sun's indwelling God
In Fire's abounding love.

GEISTIGE KOMMUNION

Es nahet mir im Erdenwirken,
In Stoffes Abbild mir gegeben,
Der Sterne Himmelswesen:
Ich seh' im Wollen sie sich liebend wandeln.

Es dringen in mich im Wasserleben,
In Stoffes Kraftgewalt mich bildend,
Der Sterne Himmelstaten:
Ich seh' im Fühlen sie sich weise wandeln.

SPIRITUAL COMMUNION

In Earth-activity draws near to me,
Given to me in substance-imaged form,
The heavenly Being of the Stars.
In Willing I see them transformed with Love.

In Watery life stream into me,
Forming me through with power of substance-force,
The heavenly Deeds of the Stars.
In Feeling I see them transformed with Wisdom.

Ich suche im Innern
Der schaffenden Kräfte Wirken,
Der schaffenden Mächte Leben.
Es sagt mir
Der Erde Schweremacht
Durch meiner Füsse Wort,
Es sagt mir
Der Lüfte Formgewalt
Durch meiner Hände Singen,
Es sagt mir
Des Himmels Lichteskraft
Durch meines Hauptes Sinnen,
Wie die Welt im Menschen
Spricht, singt, sinnt.

I seek within
The working of creative forces,
The life of creative powers.
Earth's gravity is telling me
Through the word of my feet,
Air's wafting forms are telling me
Through the singing of my hands,
And Heaven's light is telling me
Through the thinking of my head,
How the great World in Man
Speaks, sings and thinks.

Des Menschen Kräfte sind zweifach geartet;
Es geht ein Strom von Kräften nach innen:
Er gibt Gestalt und inner Wurzelsein;
Es geht ein Strom von Kräften nach aussen:
Er gibt das Wohlsein und Lebenslichterhellung;
Drum denke sich als leichten Lichtmenschen,
Wen die Bildekräfte des schweren
Körpermenschen plagen.

Twofold are the forces in Man.
One stream of forces goes inward:
This gives you form and inner root of being.
One stream of forces goes outward:
This gives well-being, fills you with light of life.
If then the heavy body-man, his forming forces weigh
                                                    you down
Picture yourself all-buoyant, man-of-light.

O Welten-Bilder,
Ihr schwebet heran
Aus Raumesweiten.
Ihr strebet nach mir,
Ihr dringet ein
In meines Hauptes
Denkende Kräfte.

Ihr meines Hauptes
Bildende Seelenkräfte,
Ihr erfüllet mein Eigensein,
Ihr dringet aus meinem Wesen
In die Weltenweiten
Und einigt mich selbst
Mit Weltenschaffensmächten.

World-All pictures!
From widths of Space
Ye are alighting,
Tending towards me,
Entering bounteously
Into my Head,
Into its thinking powers.

Ye, of my Head
The formative forces, forming in soul,
Filling my inner life!
Now reaching outward
Into World-distances,
Weld my own being
With World-creative powers.

So fühlen wir uns als Seelen im kosmischen Gedanken gebettet, wie wir den Gedanken, den kleinen Gedanken, den wir denken, in unserem Seelenleben gebettet fühlen.

Meditieren Sie einmal über die Idee: 'Ich denke meinen Gedanken' und 'Ich bin ein Gedanke, der von den Hierarchien des Kosmos gedacht wird.' Mein Ewiges besteht darin, dass das Denken der Hierarchien ein Ewiges ist. Und wenn ich einmal von einer Kategorie der Hierarchien ausgedacht bin, dann werde ich übergeben—wie der Gedanke des Menschen vom Lehrer an den Schüler übergeben wird—von einer Kategorie an die andere, damit diese mich in meiner ewigen, wahren Natur denke. So fühle ich mich drinnen in der Gedankenwelt des Kosmos.

Concluding words in the Lecture-Cycle
Human and Cosmic Thought

We are to feel ourselves—our human soul—
embedded in the cosmic Thought, even as we
feel the little thought which we ourselves are
thinking, embedded in our own life of soul. Try
then to meditate on this idea: 'I think my
thoughts,' and 'I am myself a Thought, thought
by the Hierarchies of the great Universe.' This
is the very essence of my eternal being. My being
is eternal, inasmuch as the Thinking of the
Hierarchies is eternal. And when one Category
among the Hierarchies has thought me out, I am
passed on—even as a human thought might be,
from teacher to pupil—passed on from one
Hierarchy to another, that the latter too may
think me in my true, eternal being. So do I
feel myself immersed in the divine Thought-
world of the Cosmos.

J

Im reinen Gedanken findest du
Das Selbst, das sich halten kann.

Wandelst zum Bilde du den Gedanken,
Erlebst du die schaffende Weisheit.

B

Verdichtest du das Gefühl zum Licht,
Offenbarst du die formende Kraft.

Verdinglichst du den Willen zum Wesen,
So schaffest du im Weltensein.

J

In pure Thinking thou dost find
The Self that can hold itself.

Transmute the Thought into Picture-life
And thou wilt know creative Wisdom.

B

Condense thy Feeling into Light:
Formative powers are revealed through thee.

Forge thy Will into deeds of Being:
So shalt thou share in World-creation.

Ruhiges Verweilen an den
Schönheiten des Lebens
Gibt der Seele Kraft des
Fühlens.
Klares Denken an die
Wahrheiten des Daseins
Bringt dem Geiste Licht des
Wollens.

Dwelling in silence on the beauties of life
Gives the soul strength of Feeling.

Thinking clearly on the truths of existence
Brings to the Spirit the light of Will.

Urselbst,
Von dem alles ausgegangen,
Urselbst,
Zu dem alles zurückkehrt,
Urselbst,
Das in mir lebt—
Zu dir strebe ich hin.

Primeval Self
From whom all things derive,
Primeval Self
To whom all things return,
Primeval Self
That in me lives:
    To Thee will I aspire.

Im Urbeginne strahlte das Licht;
Und das Licht kam aus dem Geiste;
Und ein Geist war das Licht.
Und Geist wird das Licht,
Wenn ich das Licht empfinde
Durch das Göttliche,
Das wirket in meiner Seele.

MEDITATION

In the Beginning rayed forth the Light,
And the Light sprang from the Spirit,—
A living Spirit was the Light.
And Spirit the Light will become for me
When I experience the Light
Through the gift of God
Implanted in my soul.

Im Urbeginne war Christus
Und Christus war bei den Göttern
Und ein Gott war Christus
Und in jedes Menschen Seele
Lebt des Christus Wesenheit;
So auch lebt Er in meiner Seele
Und wird mich führen
Zum Sinn meines Lebens.

MEDITATION

In the Beginning was Christ,
And Christ was with the Gods,
And a God was Christ.
Deep in each human soul
Being of Christ indwells.
In my soul too He dwells,
And He will lead me
To the true meaning of my life.

*Worte, um die Empfindung für die Heiligkeit des Schlafes zu
entwickeln, die Empfindung: der Schlaf vereinigt uns mit der
geistigen Welt.*

Ich schlafe ein.
Bis zum Aufwachen wird meine Seele
In der geistigen Welt sein.
Da wird sie der führenden Wesensmacht
Meines Erdenlebens begegnen,
Die in der geistigen Welt vorhanden ist,
Die mein Haupt umschwebt,—
Da wird sie dem Genius begegnen.
Und wenn ich aufwachen werde,
Werde ich die Begegnung
Mit dem Genius gehabt haben.
Die Flügel meines Genius
Werden herangeschlagen haben
An meine Seele.

THE HOLINESS OF SLEEP

(These words are to awaken in us a feeling of the holiness of sleep,—a feeling of the fact that sleep unites us with the Spiritual World.)

I go to sleep.
Till I awaken
My soul will be in the spiritual world,
And will there meet the higher Being
Who guides me through this earthly life—
Him who is ever in the spiritual world,
Who hovers about my head.
My soul will meet him,
Even the guiding Genius of my life.
And when I waken again
This meeting will have been.
I shall have felt the wafting of his wings.
The wings of my Genius
Will have touched my soul.

Morgens:

Im Geiste lag der Keim meines Leibes.
Und der Geist hat eingeprägt meinem Leibe
Die sinnlichen Augen,
Auf dass ich durch sie sehe
Das Licht der Körper.
Und der Geist hat eingeprägt meinem Leibe
Vernunft und Empfindung
Und Gefühl und Wille
Auf dass ich durch sie wahrnehme die Körper
Und auf sie wirke.
Im Geiste lag der Keim meines Leibes.

Abends:

In meinem Leibe liegt des Geistes Keim.
Und ich will eingliedern meinem Geiste
Die übersinnlichen Augen,
Auf dass ich durch sie schaue das Licht der Geister.
Und ich will einprägen meinem Geiste
Weisheit und Kraft und Liebe,
Auf dass durch mich wirken die Geister
Und ich werde das selbstbewusste Werkzeug
Ihrer Taten.
In meinem Leibe liegt des Geistes Keim.

MEDITATION

Morning:

In the Spirit lay the seed of my body.
And the Spirit has endowed my body
With physical eyes,
That with them I may behold
The light of the things around me.
And the Spirit has given to my body
Reason, sensation, feeling and will,
That through them I may perceive
The things around me
And work upon them.
In the Spirit lay the seed of my body.

Evening:

In my body lives the seed of the Spirit.
And I shall endow my Spirit
With supersensible eyes,
That with them I may behold
The light of the Spirit-Beings.
And I shall weld in my Spirit
Wisdom and Strength and Love,
That through me the Beings may work
And I may become
The conscious instrument of Their Deeds.
In my body lives the seed of the Spirit.

Siebenfach
Geisteslicht
Erstrahlt
Kraftverleihend
In
Mich
Wirksam ein.

MORNING MEDITATION

Sevenfold
Spirit-Light—
Bountiful,
Strengthening,
Quickening—
Into me
Pours.

Morgens:

Es dämmert die Sonne,
Es schwinden die Sterne.
Es dämmert die Seele,
Es schwinden die Träume.
Tag nimm mich auf,
Tag beschütze mich
In wandelndem Erdenleben.

Abends:

Wenn Sternenweltensein
Mein Ich ins Geistgebiet
Schlafend entrückt:
Hole ich mir Seelenkraft
Aus wirkender Weltenmacht
Zu streben geisteswärts.

MEDITATION

Morning:

The Sun is dawning,
The Stars are dwindling.
The soul is dawning,
And dreams are dwindling.
    Day, then, receive me,
    Day, then, protect me,
    Walking through earthly life.

Evening:

When starry Worlds
Transplant my sleeping I
Into the land of Spirit,
    I will draw strength of soul
    From World-creative Powers
    To strive towards the Spirit.

Abends:

Des Lichtes reine Strahlen
Zeiget mir der Welten Geist;
Der Liebe reine Wärme
Zeige mir der Welten Seele.
Gottinnigkeit
In meinem Herzen
In meinem Geist.

(Seelenruhe)

Morgens:

Vorstellung des Rosenkreuzes

In meinem Geist
In meinem Herzen
Gottinnigkeit.
Zeige mir der Welten Seele
Der Liebe reine Wärme;
Zeiget mir der Welten Geist
Des Lichtes reine Strahlen.

(Seelenruhe)

Meditation

Evening:

Clear rays of Light —
Spirit of the World, reveal to me!
Pure warmth of Love —
Soul of the World, impart to me!
Nearness to God
Be in my Heart,
Be in my Spirit.

(Inner silence)

Morning:

Picture to yourself the Rose-Cross.

Be in my Spirit,
Be in my Heart,
Nearness to God.
Soul of the World, impart to me
Pure warmth of Love!
Spirit of the World, reveal to me
Clear rays of Light!

(Inner silence)

Abends:

(1) Rückschau, vom Abend zum Morgen.

(2) Blau des Himmels mit vielen Sternen:

Fromm und ehrfürchtig
Sende ahnend in Raumesweiten
Meine Seele den fühlenden Blick.
Aufnehme dieser Blick
Und sende in meines Herzens Tiefen
Licht, Liebe, Leben,
Aus Geisteswelten.

(Seelenruhe)

Morgens:

Vorstellung des Rosenkreuzes

Was in diesem Sinnbild
Zu mir spricht
Der Welten hoher Geist,
Erfülle meine Seele
Zu aller Zeit
In allen Lebenslagen
Mit Licht, Liebe, Leben.

(Seelenruhe)

172

MEDITATION

(with instructions, as given to an individual pupil)

Evening:

>Look back on the events of the day from evening till morning.
>
>Picture the blue orb of Heaven, with the great multitude of stars:

>With silent reverence
>Into the depths of Space
>Go forth the vision of my soul,
>Thence to receive
>And pour into my heart
>Light and Love and Life
>From spiritual Worlds.
>
>   (Inner silence)

Morning:

>Picture to yourself the Rose-Cross

>What through this emblem
>The Spirit of the World
>Is speaking to my heart,—
>May it imbue my soul
>At all times,
>In all contingencies,
>With Light and Love and Life.
>
>   (Inner silence)

Abend:

Im Urbeginne war das Wort
Und das Wort war bei Gott
Und ein Gott war das Wort.
Und das Wort,
Es lebe im Herzen,
Im Herzen deines Wesens,
In deinem Ich.

Morgen:

In deinem Ich,
Im Herzen deines Wesens
Da lebe das Wort,
Das Geisteswort.
Und das Wort war bei Gott
Und ein Gott was das Wort.
Im Urbeginne war das Wort.

MEDITATION

Evening:

> In the Beginning was the Word
> And the Word was with God
> And a God was the Word.
> And the Word,
> May it dwell in thy heart,
> In the heart of thy being,—
> In thine I .

Morning:

> In thine I,
> In the heart of thy being
> There live the Word,
> The Spirit-Word.
> And the Word was with God
> And a God was the Word.
> In the Beginning was the Word.

Abends:

(1) Rückschau so, wie sie gefordert ist in *Wie erlangt man Erkenntnisse der höheren Welten:* fünf Minuten etwa.

(2) Rosenkreuz-Meditation, die etwa fünf Minuten dauert und an die sich dann weitere fünf Minuten lang schliesst:

In des Lichtes reinen Strahlen
Kann ich schauen
Aller Weisheit reine Kraft.
In des Herzens Wellenschlag
Kann ich fühlen
Alles Daseins starkes Sinnbild.
Beides will ich fühlen.

(Seelenruhe)

Morgens:

Erst Rosenkreuz-Meditation.
Dann Versenkung in den Gedanken:

Weisheit im Geiste,
Liebe in der Seele,
Kraft im Willen:
Sie geleiten mich
Und halten mich.
Ich vertraue ihnen,
Ich opfre ihnen.

(Seelenruhe)

Die Nebenübungen im Sinne von *Geheimwissenschaft.*

MEDITATION
(with instructions, as given to an individual pupil)

Evening:

    (1) Look back on the events of the day, as indicated in the book *Knowledge of the Higher Worlds.* About five minutes.

    (2) The Rose-Cross meditation,—about five minutes, and then these lines, again about five minutes:

In the clear rays of the Light
I see in purity
The fountain of all Wisdom.
In the wave-beat of the Heart
I feel in strength
The token of all Being.
Both of these will I feel.

                         (Inner silence)

Morning:

First, the Rose-Cross meditation. Then dwell upon this thought:

Wisdom in the Spirit,
Love in the Soul,
Strength in the Will:
These shall guide me,
These shall hold me.
In them I trust.
To them I give my life.

                         (Inner silence)

Supplementary exercises as given in *An Outline of Occult Science.*

MEDITATION
Given in English to an English pupil.

In the Morning:

Picture to yourself that you are in the midst of cosmic space, surrounded by Light, and that a voice comes to you from the four points of the compass (a single voice, but coming from four different directions) speaking to you:

"Be a strong I . Give thy heart to the Spirit of the World."

(Be very quiet in your soul after this meditation.)

In the Evening:

Review the day in backward order from evening till morning.

Picture to yourself that you are in the midst of cosmic space, surrounded by Darkness, and that you are speaking to the Full Moon in the East:

"I will be a strong I . I will give my heart to the Spirit of the World."

(Be very quiet in your soul after this meditation.)

Abends:

Es tritt bewusst mein Ich
Aus dem Reich der Daseinshüllen,
Zu ruhen in der Welten Wesen.
Ins Göttliche strebet es.
Gewinne Seele dieses Reich:
Des Geistes glänzend Wogenmeer
Des Lichts erstrahlende Gebilde.

Morgens:

Lichterstrahlende Gebilde,
Glänzendes Wogenmeer des Geistes,
Euch verliess die Seele.
In dem Göttlichen weilte sie,
In ihm ruhte ihr Wesen.
In das Reich der Daseinshüllen
Tritt bewusst mein Ich.

MEDITATION

Evening:

Consciously mine I goes forth
Out of the realm of the veils of Being
To rest in the Being of the Worlds.
Into the Divine ascending,
Reach, oh my soul, yon realm of Being,—
The Spirit's glistening Ocean-tide,
Ever-radiant forms of Light.

Morning:

Ever-radiant forms of Light,
Glistening Ocean-tide of Spirit!
Now hath the soul departed from you.
In the Divine the soul was dwelling,
In the Divine my Being rested.
Into the realm of the veils of Being
Consciously enters mine I .

Mein Haupt trägt
Der Ruhesterne Sein.
Meine Brust birgt
Der Wandelsterne Leben.
Mein Leib west
Im Elementenwesen.
Das bin ich.

My Head bears the being
of the resting Stars.
My Breast harbours the life
of the wandering Stars.
My Body lives and moves
amid the Elements.

This am I.

Ich fühle in meinem Kopf
Warme Liebekraft.
Ich fühle in meinem Herzen
Leuchtende Gedankenmacht.
Die warme Liebekraft
Vereint sich mit der
Leuchtenden Gedankenmacht.
Davon werden stark
Meine Hände
Zu gutem menschlichem Wirken.
Ich fühle mich.

In my Head I feel
Warm fount of Love.
In my Heart I feel
Raying Light of Thought.
Now the warm fount of Love
Joins with the light of Thought,
So to make strong my Hands
For the good work of Man.
I feel me.

Ich trage Ruhe in mir,
Ich trage in mir selbst
Die Kräfte, die mich stärken.
Ich will mich erfüllen
Mit dieser Kräfte Wärme,
Ich will mich durchdringen
Mit meines Willens Macht.
Und fühlen will ich
Wie Ruhe sich ergiesst
Durch all mein Sein,
Wenn ich mich stärke,
Die Ruhe als Kraft
In mir zu finden
Durch meines Strebens Macht.

Quiet I bear within me.
I bear within myself
Forces to make me strong.
Now will I be imbued
With their glowing warmth.
Now will I fill myself
With my own will's resolve.
And I will feel the quiet
Pouring through all my being,
When by my steadfast striving
I become strong
To find within myself
The source of strength,
The strength of inner quiet.

GEBET FÜR KRANKE

O Gottesgeist erfülle mich,
Erfülle mich in meiner Seele;
Meiner Seele leihe starke Kraft,
Starke Kraft auch meinem Herzen,
Meinem Herzen, das dich sucht,
Sucht durch tiefe Sehnsucht,
Tiefe Sehnsucht nach Gesundheit,
Nach Gesundheit und Starkmut
Starkmut, der in meine Glieder strömt,
Strömt wie edles Gottgeschenk,
Gottgeschenk von dir, o Gottesgeist,
O Gottesgeist erfülle mich.

Spirit of God,
Fill Thou me,
Fill me in my soul.
To my soul give strength,
Strength also to my heart,
My heart that seeks for Thee,
Seeks Thee with earnest longing,
Longing to be whole and well,
Whole and well and full of courage,
Courage the gift from the hand of God,
Gift from Thee, O Spirit of God.
Spirit of God,
Fill Thou me.

So lang du den Schmerz erfühlest,
Der mich meidet,
Ist Christus unerkannt
Im Weltenwesen wirkend.
Denn schwach nur bleibet der Geist,
Wenn er allein im eignen Leibe
Des Leidesfühlens mächtig ist.

So long as thou dost feel the pain
Which I am spared,
The Christ unrecognized
Is working in the World.
For weak is still the Spirit
While each is only capable of suffering
Through his own body.

Du meines Erdenraumes Geist,
Enthülle deines Alters Licht
Der Christ-begabten Seele,
Dass strebend sie finden kann
Im Chor der Friedenssphären
Dich, tönend von Lob und Macht
Des Christ-ergebnen Menschensinns.

Spirit of mine earthly habitation!
Reveal the Light of thine Age
To the Christ-endowèd soul,
That striving I may find thee
In the choirs of the Spheres of Peace
Singing the glory and the power
Of human hearts devoted to the Christ.

Aus des Geistes lichten Höhen
Erstrahle Gottes helles Licht
In Menschenseelen
Die suchen wollen
Des Geistes Gnade
Des Geistes Kraft
Des Geistes Sein.
Er lebe
Im Herzen,
Im Seelen-Innern
Unserer
Die wir
In Seinem Namen
Hier uns versammelt fühlen.

From the luminous heights of the Spirit
May God's clear light ray forth
Into those human souls
Who are intent on seeking
The grace of the Spirit,
The light of the Spirit,
The life of the Spirit.
May He live
In the hearts,
In the inmost souls
Of those of us
Who feel ourselves gathered together here
In His Name.

Ich schaue in die Finsternis.
In ihr erstehet Licht,
Lebendes Licht.
Wer ist dies Licht in der Finsternis?
Ich bin es selbst in meiner Wirklichkeit.
Diese Wirklichkeit des Ich
Tritt nicht ein in mein Erdensein,
Ich bin nur Bild davon.
Ich werde es aber wiederfinden
Wenn ich guten Willens für den Geist
Durch des Todes Pforte geschritten.

MEDITATION

I gaze into the darkness.
In it there arises Light—
Living Light.
Who is this Light in the darkness?
It is I myself in my reality.
This reality of the I
Enters not into my earthly life;
I am but a picture of it.
But I shall find it again
When with good will for the Spirit
I shall have passed through the Gate of Death.

Alles, was da lebt im Weltenall,
Es lebt nur, indem zu neuem Leben
Es den Keim in sich erschafft.
Und die Seele, sie ergibt
Dem Altern sich nur und dem Tode,
Um unsterblich zu stets neuem Leben
Heranzureifen.

All things alive throughout the Universe
Live but in bringing forth within them
The seed of a new life.
So too the soul of Man is given up
To ageing and to death,
Only that deathless he may ripen
To ever newly resurrected life.

Im Wollen kommender Erdentage
Erstehen, stark zum schaffenden Leben,
Die Kräfte, die—hingetragen
Durchs Tor des Todes und Erdenleidens—
Im Geiste sicher leuchten und wärmen.

In künft'gen Erdentagen, wenn friedevoll
Des Geistes Wirken durch das Erdental
Die Offenbarung seiner Willenskraft
Durch Menschenseelen heilsam tragen wird,
Dann wird in Menschen als Daseinskraft
Der edle Wille leben, der die Opfertat
Am Todestore treu vollbringt.

In willing of future earthly days
There shall arise, strong to creative life,
Forces of good, which—carried through the gate
Of earthly death and pain—
Give certain Light and Warmth in Spirit-land.

In future earthly days, when peacefully
The Spirit, working through the vale of Earth,
Will bear the revelation of His power of Will
With grace and healing through the souls of men,
Then will there live in man—his inmost strength of being—
The noble will, which faithfully fulfils
The deed of sacrifice at the Gate of Death.

Aus dem Mut der Kämpfer,
Aus dem Blut der Schlachten,
Aus dem Leid Verlassener,
Aus des Volkes Opfertaten
Wird erwachsen Geistesfrucht,
Lenken Seelen geistbewusst
Ihren Sinn ins Geisterreich.

From the courage of the fighters,
From the blood on fields of battle,
From the grief of the bereaved,
From the people's sacrifice:
There will ripen fruit of Spirit,
If souls will turn in consciousness
Towards the realm of Spirit.

Geister Eurer Seelen, wirkende Wächter,
Eure Schwingen mögen bringen
Unsrer Seelen bittende Liebe
Eurer Hut vertrauten Erdenmenschen;
Dass, mit Eurer Macht geeint,
Unsre Bitte helfend strahle
Den Seelen, die sie liebend sucht.

Geister Eurer Seelen, wirkende Wächter,
Eure Schwingen mögen bringen
Unsrer Seelen bittende Liebe
Eurer Hut vertrauten Sphärenmenschen;
Dass, mit Eurer Macht geeint,
Unsre Bitte helfend strahle
Den Seelen, die sie liebend sucht.

For friends on Earth, especially for those in danger

Spirits ever watchful, Guardians of your souls,
May your pinions carry
Our souls' petitioning love
To the human beings upon Earth committed to your care;
That, united with your power,
Our prayer may radiate with help
To the souls whom our love is seeking.

For friends who have gone through the Gate of Death

Spirits ever watchful, Guardians of your souls,
May your pinions carry
Our souls' petitioning love
To the human beings in the Spheres committed to your care;
That, united with your power,
Our prayer may radiate with help
To the souls whom our love is seeking.

Es empfangen Angeloi, Archangeloi, Archai
Im Aetherweben,
Das Schicksalsnetz des Menschen.

Es verwesen in Exusiai, Dynamis, Kyriotetes,
Im Astralempfinden des Kosmos,
Die gerechten Folgen des Erdenlebens des Menschen.

Es auferstehen in Thronen, Cherubim, Seraphim,
Als deren Tatenwesen,
Die gerechten Ausgestaltungen
    des Erdenlebens des Menschen.

Angels, Archangels and Archai
in the Ether weaving,
receive man's web of Destiny.

In Exusiai, Dynamis and Kyriotetes,
in the astral feeling of the Cosmos,
the just consequences of the earthly life of man
    die into the realm of Being.

In Thrones and Cherubim and Seraphim,
as Their Deeds of Being,
the justly transmuted fruits of the earthly life of man
    are resurrected.

Im Lichte der Weltgedanken,
Da webet die Seele, die
Vereint mit mir auf Erden.

Meines Herzens warmes Leben,
Es ströme zu deiner Seele hin,
Zu wärmen deine Kälte,
Zu sänftigen deine Hitze.

In den Geisteswelten
Mögen leben meine Gedanken in deinen,
Und deine Gedanken in meinen.

In Light of Cosmic Thoughts
Now weaves the soul
That was united with me upon Earth.

May the warm life of my heart
Stream outward to thy soul
To warm thy cold
And mitigate thy heat.
In spiritual worlds
May my thoughts live in thine
And thy thoughts live in mine.

14—VAM

Ich schaue auf Dich in der geistigen Welt,
In der Du bist.
Meine Liebe lindre Deine Wärme,
Meine Liebe lindre Deine Kälte.
Sie dringe zu Dir und helfe Dir
Zu finden den Weg
Durch des Geistes Dunkel
In des Geistes Licht.

I gaze upon thee
In the spiritual World
In which thou art.
May my love mitigate thy warmth,
May my love mitigate thy cold,
May it reach out to thee and help thee
To find thy way
Through Spirit-darkness
To Spirit-light.

Es strebe zu dir meiner Seele Liebe,
Es ströme zu dir meiner Liebe Sinn.
Sie mögen dich tragen,
Sie mögen dich halten
In Hoffnungshöhen,
In Liebessphären.

Upward to thee strive the love of my soul,
Upward to thee flow the stream of my love!
    May they sustain thee,
    May they enfold thee
    In heights of Hope,
    In spheres of Love.

In Geistgefilde will ich senden
Die treue Liebe, die wir fanden,
Um Seele mit der Seele zu verbinden.
Du sollst mein Denken liebend finden,
Wenn aus des Geistes lichten Landen
Du suchend wirst die Seele wenden,
Zu schauen, was in mir du suchest.

Into the fields of Spirit will I send
The faithful love we found on Earth,
Uniting soul with soul.
And thou wilt find my loving thought
When from the Spirit-lands of light
Thou hither turn thy seeking soul
To find what thou dost seek in me.

Herzensliebe dringe zu Seelenliebe,
Liebewärme strahle zu Geisteslicht.
So nahen wir uns euch
Denkend mit euch Geistgedanken,
Fühlend in euch Weltenliebe,
Geistig-wollend durch euch
Eins-Erleben seiend weben.

May love of hearts reach out to love of souls,
May warmth of love ray out to Spirit-light.
Even so would we draw near to you,
Thinking with you Thoughts of Spirit,
Feeling in you the Love of Worlds,
Consciously at one with you
Willing in silent Being.

In Menschenseelen will ich lenken
Das Geistgefühl, dass willig es
Das Osterwort im Herzen wecke;

Mit Menschengeistern will ich denken
Die Seelenwärme, dass kräftig sie
Den Auferstand'nen fühlen können;

Es leuchtet hell dem Todesscheine
Des Geisteswissens Erdenflamme;
Das Selbst wird Welten-Aug' und -Ohr.

Into the souls of men will I guide
The feeling for the Spirit, that willingly
The Easter Word may waken in their hearts.

And in communion with their spirit will I think
In warmth of soul, that strongly they be able
To feel the Risen Christ.

Kindled on Earth, the flame of spiritual knowledge
Irradiates the phantom light of Death.
The Self becomes World-eye and -ear.

Ich war mit euch vereint,
Bleibet in mir vereint.
Wir werden zusammen sprechen
In der Sprache des ewigen Seins.
Wir werden tätig sein,
Da wo der Taten Ergebnis wirkt.
Wir werden weben im Geiste,
Da wo gewoben werden Menschen-Gedanken
Im Wort der ew'gen Gedanken.

I was united with you.
Stay now united in me.
So shall we speak together
In the language of eternal Being.
So shall we work together
Where deeds find their fulfilment.
So shall we weave in the Spirit
Where human thoughts are woven
In the Word of eternal Thought.

Der Christus kennt uns. —Ich könnte nichts Esoterischeres geben für die unsere Geisteswissenschaft im richtigen Licht erblickende Seele und für das im rechten Sinne die Geisteswissenschaft fühlende Herz, als das Wort:

Der Christus sieht uns.

Christ knows us. To a soul that sees our Spiritual Science in the true light, to a heart that feels it in its true significance, I can impart no more esoteric saying:

The Christ is seeing us.

NOTES AND REFERENCES

1 (page 129). *At the turning-point of Time . . .*

This is the concluding verse of the meditation known as the "Foundation Stone" of the Anthroposophical Society, given on Christmas Day, 1923, printed in full in the volume *The Foundation Stone* (1957); also in *Anthroposophical Leading Thoughts* (1927). Having imparted and explained the first three verses, Rudolf Steiner spoke the following words while leading up to the concluding verse: "We do this at a moment when the remembering of man who truly understands the world looks back to the turning-point in mankind's evolution, the turning-point of Time, when amid darkness of night—darkness in moral feeling of mankind—striking in as light from Heaven there was born the Divine Being who became the Christ, the Spirit-Being who came to dwell in mankind. And we can best make strong the warmth of soul and light of soul we need, if quickened and inspired by that warmth and light which rayed forth at the turning-point of Time, even the Light of Christ amid the darkness of the world. The original Christmas . . . two thousand years ago—let us now call it to life in our own heart and mind and will. . . . So let the feeling of our hearts be turned backward in time to the first Christmas Night in ancient Palestine."

2 (pages 74–77).

The mantric sayings printed on these pages are from the course of four lectures: *Easter: a Chapter in the Mystery Wisdom of Man*, given by Dr. Steiner at

Dornach, 19th to 22nd April, 1924. For an adequate explanation, a thorough study of these lectures— available in book form—is essential. The following is but a brief indication of the theme.

Stand in the porch at Man's life-entrance. . . . The three couplets of this mantric saying express the threefold mystery: of Birth, of spiritual Re-birth during earthly life, and of Death, seen as the Birth of the soul into the coming life in spiritual worlds.

Offspring of all the Worlds! Shortly before his final descent to Earth from cosmic spiritual worlds, the soul of Man is among the spiritual Beings of the Lunar sphere, and is there enabled to form his Etheric Body— in its essence a body of cosmic light—for the coming incarnation, receiving into it according to his Karma the spiritual virtues of the seven Planets. In the Ephesian Mysteries, says Rudolf Steiner, this experience of the pre-natal life was re-awakened. The words express how in the forming of his Ether-body Man is seen from the great Universe as a form of light, united with the whole planetary system and with the bounty of the cosmic Ether, by which the life of Nature too is renewed from year to year.

3   (page 91). *O Man, thou mouldest it to thy service. . .*

Reference is here made to the iron, by means of which man has been able to create the industrial civilization of modern time. Rudolf Steiner speaks of it in relation to the meteoric iron, entering the Earth's atmosphere from the Cosmos in the showers of meteorites, in the late summer when Michaelmas is drawing near. Akin to this is the iron in man's blood, described as a healing and clarifying power in the human Microcosm. "Michael's sword" is the spiritual counterpart of the material use and value of the iron, which have alone been considered until now.

In the lecture in which a full explanation will be found (Dornach, 5th October, 1923), Rudolf Steiner continued with the words: ". . . when to thee is revealed the Power sublime of its indwelling Spirit— namely the Power of Michael, whose sword is fused and welded in the world-wide spaces from the meteoric iron. For this will be revealed to man when he is able to spiritualize the power which iron has hitherto been bringing to his material civilization. For it will then be transmuted into the strong iron of Michael, rousing and awakening the mere Nature-consciousness of modern man to consciousness of spiritual Selfhood."

4 (page 153). *In pure thinking thou dost find* . . .

These verses call for a fuller and partly historical explanation. In the year 1907 Rudolf Steiner published the collection *Occult Seals and Columns*, with an accompanying text. The pictures, based on his sketches and instructions, have been drawn and re-drawn by a number of artists from time to time. In the English edition (published in 1924) they are by Arild Rosen-krantz. On a far larger scale, the seven Seals and Columns decorated the Lecture Hall at the Congress of European Sections of the Theosophical Society, held in 1907 at Munich, where Rudolf Steiner and his pupils were responsible for the arrangements.

The seven Seals have an obvious, though not always direct relation to the great Imaginative pictures in the Apocalypse of St. John. (Some of them, Dr. Steiner acknowledges, will also be found—though with modi-

227

fications—in the occult literature of more recent times.) The designs on the seven Columns were afterwards reproduced in fully plastic form in the great wooden pillars supporting the large dome of the first Goetheanum.

The fourth Seal, which especially concerns us here, is related to the 10th Chapter of the Apocalypse:

"And I saw another mighty angel come down from heaven, clothed with a cloud; and a rainbow was upon his head, and his face was as it were the sun, and his feet as pillars of fire:

"And he had in his hand a little book open: and he set his right foot upon the sea, and his left foot on the earth. . . .

"And the voice which I heard from heaven spake with me again, and said, Go and take the little book which is open in the hand of the angel which standeth upon the sea and upon the earth.

"And I went unto the angel and said unto him, Give me the little book. And he said unto me, Take it and eat it up; and it shall make thy belly bitter, but it shall be in thy mouth sweet as honey.

"And I took the little book out of the angel's hand, and ate it up; and it was in my mouth sweet as honey: and as soon as I had eaten it, my belly was bitter."

The fourth Seal, as shown by Rudolf Steiner, pictures the "angel clothed with a cloud, a rainbow upon his head, his face as it were the sun, and his feet as pillars of fire, his right foot set upon the sea and his left foot on the earth". But the twin pillars are shown as architectural columns. The right-hand one (that is, the one on the left as seen by the onlooker) is planted in the sea; the left-hand one (seen on the right) on a rocky promontory. Written as if in letters of fire, the pillars bear the initial letters J and B respectively.

In addition, in the Congress Hall at Munich, to the left and right of the proscenium, two actual pillars were erected, surmounted by spheres, and bearing the same initials J and B, beneath which were inscribed on either hand the verses reproduced in the original on page 152. Rudolf Steiner gives the following explanations (quoted from *Occult Seals and Columns* and from the lecture given at Munich, 21st May, 1907).

"In the fourth Seal we see the Pillars, one of them planted in the sea, the other on dry land. These Pillars indicate the secret of the part played in human evolution by the red blood, rich in oxygen, and the blue or bluish-red, rich in carbonic acid. The evolution of the I of man during the Earth-epoch finds physical expression in the interaction between the red blood, without which there could be no *Life*, and the blue, without which there could be no *Knowledge*. Blue blood is the physical expression of those forces which give us Knowledge—forces which, however, taken by themselves and in their human form, are very nearly akin to Death. Red blood is the physical expression of Life—which, however, in its human form and by itself, could never give us conscious Knowledge. Together and in their mutual interaction they represent the Tree of Knowledge and the Tree of Life, or the two pillars on the foundation of which the life and cognition of the I can grow and develop to that degree of maturity where at long last man will be fully united with the universal forces of the Earth."

229

"The Initiate foresees a future condition of mankind in which the Tree of Knowledge and the Tree of Life . . . will be intertwined and united within man himself. At the present stage the aspirant to spiritual development should inscribe the message of the two pillars in his heart. Separated though they still are, they summon us to transcend the present state of mankind and to direct our footsteps to the place where through our widened consciousness the two will be interwoven—a secret that is indicated in the J——B. The verses inscribed on either pillar will bring home to us their meaning. Those on the first pillar relate to Knowledge, those on the second to Life itself. Thus at the former stage the formative, creative powers are revealed to man; at the latter he himself reveals them, magically. Progression from the mere faculty of cognition to that of magical activity in life is the significance of the transition from the power latent in the first inscription to that which is latent in the second."

In another form, Rudolf Steiner touched upon this theme in a lecture he gave in London on 17th November, 1922 (published in the booklet *First Steps in Supersensible Perception*, and *The Relation of Anthroposophy to Christianity*). Here he put forward side by side the conceptions of "exact clairvoyance" and of "ideal magic". The former means clairvoyance accompanied by such conscious thought and discriminating insight that the Imaginative picture-world becomes a means of objective knowledge. This Dr. Steiner described as the due outcome of the transmutation of Thinking on the path of higher knowledge. "Ideal

230

magic" is the faculty resulting from the transmutation of the Will.

The successive stages on the path of knowledge, set forth in Dr. Steiner's *Knowledge of Higher Worlds*, in his *Occult Science* and in his general theory of knowledge, are indeed clearly recognisable in the four couplets inscribed on the pillars J and B. Within the prevailing consciousness of the present age, pure Thinking is or at least *can be* attained, enabling man to find himself—to "come into his own", in spiritual freedom. From this secure starting-point, along the path of knowledge Thinking can be transmuted into the living picture-world of "Imagination". But at this stage man is not yet at one with the spiritual reality, the living impressions of which he is receiving. The transmutation of Feeling and Will leads on to the higher stages known as "Inspiration" and "Intuition". Sublime in their fulfilment, these deeper changes can only be the outcome of sacrifice; along the arduous pathway they involve spiritual suffering and forgoing. The little book that was sweet as honey in the mouth becomes bitter in the belly.

It is only at these higher stages that Man becomes fully at one with spiritual Being. He has progressed from the perception, from the cognition of the spiritual, to the condition in which he himself is actively partaking in the creative powers of the World.

5   (page 135). *The Mystery of the Way of God can now be known* . . .

(Translation from I. Timothy, ch. 3, verse 16.) In the lecture in which Rudolf Steiner gave this rendering, he was giving general advice for the meditative life.

He introduced the passage somewhat as follows: "There are many potent themes for meditation, especially in the Bible. Among these may be mentioned: the Words of Creation in the opening chapters of Genesis; the many sublime moments in the life of Moses, such as the manifestation of Jahve in the burning bush; the Gospel narratives; the opening words of St. John's Gospel, and sayings of the Christ, for example: 'I am the Light of the World'. Another very effective theme for meditation is a passage in I. Timothy, chapter 3, verse 16, in the following translation."

6 (page 179). *Meditation given in English*

It was at Ilkley in 1923 that Rudolf Steiner gave this meditation to an individual pupil, rendering it into English directly with the occasional help of an interpreter who was also present. In answer to questions, he explained: For the world of Mankind 'the Spirit of the World' signifies the Christ. For Nature, it signifies the Father-God. For resurrected Man, it signifies the Holy Spirit. He also said: the Full Moon in the East represents the Spirit of the World for sleeping Man.

7 (page 191). *So long as thou dost feel the pain . . .*

Speaking at Berlin on 1st September, 1914, Rudolf Steiner introduced this verse with the following words:
"How often may the near future bring us the opportunities of testing whether the Christ is truly living in us—the Christ who works across from our own heart into the hearts of our fellows, making us one with our suffering fellow-men. . . Many of us will no doubt soon be placed where the events of our time bring

suffering in their train. We shall be able to test whether we are strong enough to feel another's pain—whether the pain, living in the other soul, can become pain which we ourselves are feeling. That mankind may gradually come to this—that the pain in which another has to live does not leave us aside, but lives also in ourselves—to this end too the blood of Christ flowed on the hill of Golgotha. In the times that are now upon us let us then try to strengthen in our souls this inner mood, as we may do with the help of the following words. We speak them silently within ourselves as often as we can, when pondering the grave events of the present time. With the first line our thoughts are turned to our suffering fellow-man." (Quoted from *Thoughts for the Times*, lecture 1.)

8   (page 193). *Spirit of mine earthly habitation* . . .

This is a meditative prayer addressed to the Nation-soul—the guiding Archangel of the people to whom one belongs. Given shortly after the outbreak of war in 1914, it soon became known and used by Dr. Steiner's pupils in all countries.

It is characteristic that in the first line, the Archangel is addressed "Du meines Erden*raumes* Geist" (literally, "Thou Spirit of mine earthly *space*".) Rudolf Steiner emphasized how the Nation-soul is united with the whole atmosphere and mood of the landscape, the cosmic spiritual forces of Nature in the given country. Often he would lay stress on this, not only on the hereditary aspect of nationality. Referring to the primeval *origin* of racial and national differentiations, he wrote in 1925 (*The Michael Mystery*, Ch. XVIII): "The forces of the Stars impinge upon the different

233

regions of the Earth in different ways, in diverse constellations. Thus on the Earth—in the distribution of land and water, in the climate, in the growth of plants and so on—the starry Heavens too are living. The human being has to adapt himself to these celestial influences upon Earth. This adaptation is an essential element in his etheric body, the differentiated form of which is the original creation of the Archangeloi—that is, the whole choir of the Archangeloi together."

Rudolf Steiner also explained the expression "the light of thine Age" in the second line: "In the language of Spiritual Science the inmost essence or essential nature of a spiritual Being is referred to as his 'age'. The 'Age' of a spiritual Being signifies what that Being truly is. You will remember how we have learned to characterize the spiritual Beings according to their age in cosmic evolution."—The meaning of this line is therefore: "Reveal the light of thy true Being". (*Thoughts for the Times*, Berlin, 1914, lecture 1.)

9 (page 205). *Spirits ever watchful . . .*

These verses were originally given during the War of 1914–18, thinking of those at the front, and those who had already fallen. Lecturing to Groups of the Anthroposophical Society at the time, Rudolf Steiner made a practice of beginning with these (or other equivalent) verses, introducing them somewhat as follows: "Let our first thoughts again be turned to those who are out on the battlefields amid the stern events of our time; also to those who in consequence of these events have already passed through the gate of death." After the repetition of the verses he would continue: "And the Spirit whom in our spiritual

movement we have been seeking for these many years—
the Spirit who went through the Mystery of Golgotha,
who is the Spirit of courage and fortitude, the Spirit
who unites mankind, even the Spirit of Peace—may
He be with you amid your arduous duties."

Like other meditative sayings given in connection
with the War (pp. 190–193, 202–203), these verses soon
became known in all the countries where there were
Groups of the Anthroposophical Society. Translated
into English and other languages, here too they were
regularly used at the opening of Group Meetings.

Answering questions that had been asked, Rudolf
Steiner said that the words could also be used in the
singular, both with respect to the one who speaks or
thinks them and with respect to the one on whose
behalf they are uttered. They can be spoken by many
on behalf of one, by one on behalf of many, and so on.
For example, the first of the two verses as printed on
p. 205 can be replaced by the following:

Spirit ever watchful, Guardian of thy soul!
May thy pinions carry
My soul's petitioning love
To the human being upon Earth committed to thy
care;
That, united with thy power,
My prayer may radiate with help
To the soul whom my love is seeking.

Dr. Steiner had also been asked about the repetition
of the "your" (or the "thy") in the first two lines. For in
the first, the word is evidently addressed to the human
souls, and in the second to their Guardian Spirits. In
answer he said that words received from the spiritual
world sometimes present inevitable difficulties as to

grammatical structure. This was one of several occasions on which he pointed out that the more rigid categories of earthly logic, implicit in the conventional rules of grammar and syntax, cannot invariably be maintained in spiritual realms. (Compare *Thoughts for the Times*, Berlin, 1914–15, lectures 1, 2 and 5.)

10   (page 207). *Angels, Archangels and Archai . . .*

In the lecture in which these three sentences were given, Rudolf Steiner described how in the three successive stages of the life after death the spiritual Hierarchies progressively receive and transmute the fruits of man's earthly life. Expressing it in these meditative sayings, he recommended the practice of thinking thus concretely about the Dead. "We utter a simple and good, a wonderful and beautiful prayer, when we think of the connection of life and death, or of one who has passed through the gate of death, in this way. Much depends upon it, whether human beings on earth *think* the spiritual facts or not: whether they merely accompany the Dead with thoughts that remain behind on earth, or accompany them on their further path with thoughts that are a true image of what takes place in yonder realm which they have entered. . . . Therefore human hearts should be ready to hear once more, what human hearts *did* hear in the Mysteries and Initiation-centres of olden time when they called out impressively, again and again to those who were about to be initiated:—'Accompany the Dead in their further Destinies!'"

The three sentences may also be spoken or meditated on behalf of an individual soul. Then the words "man's web of destiny" can be replaced by "thy web of destiny", and the words "the earthly life of man" by "thy earthly life",—or the name of the departed may be inserted.

The lecture here quoted (Dornach, 4th July, 1924) is No. 2 in the volume *Karmic Relationships: Esoteric Studies*, vol. III (or—in the earlier edition—*The Karmic Relationships of the Anthroposophical Movement*.)

11 (page 217). *May Love of hearts . . .*

This meditation too may be used in the singular, replacing the *we* and *you* by *I* and *thee*, or the one or other as the case may be. (Compare Notes 9 and 10.)

12 (page 219). *Into the souls of men . . .*

Rudolf Steiner frequently spoke at the burial or cremation of members of the Anthroposophical Society. From his perception of the soul who had passed on into spiritual worlds, he sometimes expressed in rhythmic form what he perceived as that individual's experience, looking back on the earthly life now completed and forward into the future.

These are the last three of nine verses spoken in this way in memory of L. Grossheintz, who died in January 1915.

13 (page 221). *I was united with you . . .*

See the preceding Note.

These lines were spoken at the cremation of Georga Wiese. Rudolf Steiner introduced them with the words: "It is to me as though she were now speaking to us, down from the realms of light."

237

BIBLIOGRAPHY

I. In English translation.

Among Rudolf Steiner's written works, the following deal especially with the path of knowledge, and with meditation:

Knowledge of the Higher Worlds and its Attainment.
(Earlier editions of this book were in two volumes, entitled *The Way of Initiation* and *Initiation and its Results*.)
Stages of Higher Knowledge
A Road to Self-Knowledge in Eight Meditations
The Threshold of the Spiritual World
Calendar of the Soul. Verses for the fifty-two weeks of the year.

The following fundamental works also contain chapters on the path of knowledge:
Theosophy: an Introduction to the Supersensible Knowledge of the World and the Destination of Man
An Outline of Occult Science. (Attention is especially drawn to the long chapter entitled: "Knowledge of Higher Worlds—Initiation".)
Four Mystery Plays
The Foundation Stone (Dornach, Christmas 1923)
Anthroposophical Leading Thoughts
The Michael Mystery

Among Rudolf Steiner's numerous lectures and lecture-courses now available in book form, the following may especially be mentioned. (Many others are referred to in the Index.)
The Theosophy of the Rosicrucian (Lecture-Course, Munich, June-July 1907)

239

The Gospel of St. John (Lecture-Course, Hamburg, May 1908)

The Effect of Occult Development upon the Self and the Sheaths of Man (Lecture-Course, the Hague, March 1913)

Anthroposophy: an Introduction (Lecture-Course, Dornach, January-February 1924)

The Lord's Prayer (Berlin, 28.I.1907)

Practical Training in Thought (Carlsruhe, 18.I.1909)

Paths to Knowledge of the Higher Worlds (Oslo, 26.XI.1921)

Meditation and Concentration. The three forms of Clairvoyance (Dornach, 27.III.1915)

Knowledge and Initiation (London, 14–15.IV.1922)

The Change in the Path to Supersensible Knowledge (Dornach, 17.V.1922)

First Steps in Supersensible Perception (London, 17–18.XI.1922)

On the Festivals of the Year:
Festivals and their Meaning

    Vol. I.   *Christmas* (8 lectures, 1905–1921)

    Vol. II.   *Easter* (8 lectures, 1908–1922)

    Vol. III.   *Ascension and Pentecost* (7 lectures, 1908–1924)

    Vol. IV.   *Michaelmas* (4 lectures and extracts, 1913–1924)

The Four Seasons and the Archangels (5 lectures, Dornach, October 1923)

The Cycle of the Year (5 lectures, Dornach, March–April 1923)

Easter: a Chapter in the Mystery Wisdom of Man (4 lectures, Dornach, April 1924)

The following include advice concerning meditation for the Dead:

Thoughts for the Times (Lecture-Course, Berlin, 1914–1915)

Earthly Death and Cosmic Life (Lecture-Course, Berlin, March 1918)

The Inner Nature of Man and the Life between Death and a new Birth (Lecture-Course, Vienna, April 1914)

Links between the Living and the Dead and *The Transformation of Earthly Forces into Clairvoyance* (Bergen, 10–11.X.1913)

II. In the Original.

In addition to the originals of the above, the following should be mentioned:

Wahrspruchworte. New and comprehensive edition, 1961. This contains the originals of most of the verses published in the present volume.

Rudolf Steiner und unsere Toten (1935). This contains meditations for the Dead, a few of which are reproduced in the present volume; also lectures and addresses in which Rudolf Steiner speaks of the life after death and gives practical advice concerning the relation of the living to the dead.

The verses and meditations reproduced on pages 46, 158–160, 166, 170–179, 182–184 and 194 are published here for the first time.

INDEX
of first lines in German

INDEX
of first lines in English

252